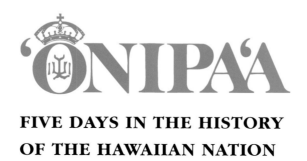

'ONIPA'A

FIVE DAYS IN THE HISTORY
OF THE HAWAIIAN NATION

CONTRIBUTING WRITERS

R-M. Keahi Allen
James Bartels
Cobey Black
Glen Grant
Victoria Kneubuhl
Elizabeth Pa Martin
Eloise Ululani Tungpalan
Palani Vaughan

CONTRIBUTING PHOTOGRAPHERS

Monica Weckman Albert
Bruce Asato
Debra Booker
Steve Brinkman
Joseph Chang
Jeff Clark
Holly Henderson
Russell Ho
Ken Ige
Kai Joger
Eileen Kalāhiki
Craig Kojima
Lani Ma'a Lapilio
Robb Loo
Kendra Lucht
David Martin
Deborah Pope

Elizabeth Pa Martin
Annelore Niejahr
Dennis Oda
Douglas Peebles
Rod Thompson
Mike Tsukamoto
Deborah Uchida
Take Umeda
Carl Viti
Deborah Ward
Gregory Yamamoto

Bishop Museum
Friends of 'Iolani Palace
Hawai'i State Archives
Judiciary History Center
Kukui Foundation

FIVE DAYS IN THE HISTORY OF THE HAWAIIAN NATION

Centennial Observance of the Overthrow of the Hawaiian Monarchy

GLOSSARY

'āina: land.

'ahahui: society.

ahu: an altar or shrine.

akua: gods.

ali'i: a chief or chiefess; of noble or royal birth.

ali'i 'aimoku: a chief who rules an island or district.

aloha: love, affection; a greeting of affection.

'aumākua: family ancestors, deities.

'awa: a shrub, the root being the source of a drink of the same name used in ceremonies.

'awapuhi: fragrant ginger

ea: sovereignty, rule, independence.

ha'i 'ōlelo: speaker.

haka: platform.

haka lele: altar.

hala: the pandanus or screwpine, the yellow to red fruit sections are used for *leis*.

haole: white person, Caucasian; formerly any foreigner.

heiau: a Hawaiian temple or place of worship of pre-Christian origin.

holokū: mu'u mu'u with yoke and train.

ho'okupu: ceremonial gift-giving as a sign of honor and respect.

hula: dance, to dance.

hālau hula: a *hula* troupe, also a place of *hula* instruction.

'ilima: a small native shrub whose delicate flowers are strung for *lei*, about 500 flowers are needed for one *lei*.

'ike pono: to know definitely and see clearly.

kāhili: a feather standard symbolic of royalty.

kahu: a guardian, honored attendant or keeper.

kahuna: a priest, minister or sorcerer; an expert in any profession.

kamali'i: children.

kanaka maoli: native people

kanikau: a dirge, lamentation or chant of mourning.

kapu: taboo, prohibition; special privilege; sacred, holy.

keiki: child, offspring, descendant.

kīhei: cape, shawl or cloak.

kuhina nui: prime minister, premier; an officer of the early monarchy who shared executive power with the king.

kukunaokalā: calyx of a mangrove as used in making *lei*; mangrove.

kulāiwi: native land.

kumu hula: *hula* instructor; *hula* expert.

kumulipo: creation chant.

kūpe'e: bracelet, anklet.

kupuna: grandparent, ancestor, elder.

kūpuna: plural *kupuna*.

lauhala: leaves of the pandanus, used for weaving.

lei: a garland or wreath, given as a sign of affection.

lei 'a'i: neck lei

lei aloha: a *lei* given with special love and affection.

lei hulu: feather *lei*, formerly worn by royalty.

lei ho'okupu: a *lei* given as a ceremonial offering.

lei po'o: head lei.

maile: a native twining shrub with fragrant leaves used for *leis* and decoration.

maka'āinana: commoner, the populace, people in general.

mana: divine power, miraculous or supernatural power, a spiritual force.

mu'umu'u: a loose fitting island dress patterned after the Mother Hubbards of the missionaries.

na'au: gut, center of emotions

nā kānaka maoli: the true people, the indigenous people.

nā pua: the flowers; the children, descendants, offspring.

niho palaoa: a whale tooth pendant and symbol of royalty.

oli: a chant not danced to.

oli kapu: a sacred chant.

'onipa'a: steadfast, firm, immovable.

pahu: a drum.

pīkake: the Arabian jasmine, introduced from India, whose fragrant flowers are used for *lei* peacock.

pōhaku: rock or stone; thunder.

pono: goodness, uprightness, excellence and well-being.

pūlo'ulo'u: a tapa-covered ball on a stick carried before a chief as a symbol of sacredness.

'ukulele: a stringed instrument brought to Hawai'i by the Portuguese.

'umeke: bowl, calabash, circular vessel of wood or gourd.

Copyright ©1994 Office of Hawaiian Affairs, 711 Kapi'olani Boulevard, Suite 500, Honolulu, Hawai'i 96813

ISBN 1-56647-051-X

Design:
Michael Horton Design

First Printing August 1994
1 2 3 4 5 6 7 8 9

Prepress and printing of this volume was through the book packaging program of Mutual Publishing.

Printed in Singapore

'ONIPA'A CENTENNIAL COMMITTEE

Attending a January 1993 meeting: 1st row—Rev. William Kaina, Betty Lou Stroup, Melvin Kalāhiki, Sen. Eloise Ululani Tungpalan, Keiji Kawakami, Wendell Silva; 2nd row—Lilinoe Lindsey, Apolei Bargamento (OHA staff), Kamaki A. Kanahele III, Palani Vaughan; 3rd row—Wendy Roylo Hee, Rowena Akana, James Bartels, R-M. Keahi Allen, Elizabeth Pa Martin, and Momi Cazimero. (Russell Ho photo)

Senator Eloise Ululani Tungpalan, *Chair*
Francis McMillen, *Vice Chair*
Rowena N. Akana
R-M. Keahi Allen
James Bartels
Peter Ching
Momi Cazimero
Dave Chun
Senator Mike Crozier
Rockne Freitas
Mufi Hannemann
Al Harrington
Wendy Roylo Hee
Leinā'ala Heine
Rev. William Kaina
Melvin Kalāhiki
Kamaki A. Kanahele III
Edward Ka'ōpūiki
Keiji Kawakami
Lilinoe Lindsey
Elizabeth A. Ho'oipo
    Kalaena'auao Pa Martin
Robert Pfeiffer
Wendell Silva
Margaret Kula Stafford
Betty Lou Stroup
Palani Vaughan
Dallas Mossman Vogeler

ʻONIPAʻA CONTRIBUTORS

NĀ PAKELONA (PATRONS)

State of Hawaiʻi

Governor John Waiheʻe

Governor's Office of International Relations

Department of Accounting and General Services

Department of Business, Economic Development & Tourism

Hawaiʻi State Library

Hawaiʻi Visitors Bureau

Department of Hawaiian Home Lands

Department of Land & Natural Resources

Department of Transportation

State Judiciary

U.H. Office of the Vice-Pres. for University Relations

Hawaiʻi State Archives:
  State Archivist - Jolyn Tamura
  Support Service Staff - Della Mae Kuaʻana, Gloria Riingen, Jean Charbonnet, Victoria Nihi

City & County of Honolulu
  Mayor Frank F. Fasi
  Gary Gill, Chairman, City Council of Honolulu

Honolulu Police Department

Friends of ʻIolani Palace

Aaron Mahi & the Royal Hawaiian Band

Kyo-Ya Company, Ltd.

State Council on Hawaiian Heritage

Hui Naʻauao

Stanley A. Styan

Cutter Ford-Isuzu, Inc.

Thomas & Miye Yagi

Gerald Y. Sekiya

Aloha Petroleum, Ltd.

Foodland Super Market, Ltd.

First Federal Savings & Loan of America

Hannigan & Ehresman, Attorneys at Law

Hawaiʻi Educational & Cultural Society, Inc.

Hawaiʻi Fire Fighters Association - Community Relations Fund

Diane M. L. Mark

Edward J. Kormondy

Outrigger Hotels Hawaiʻi

Alexander & Baldwin Foundation

Edward A. & Betty Lou Stroup

James B. & Elizabeth M. Young

Walter Dods, Jr.

Hawaiian Electric Industries, Inc.

Bishop Museum Archives:
  Curator - Lynn Davis
  Staff Assistant - Marge Kemp

Bernard Von Nothaus (Royal Hawaiian Mint)

Larry Mehau (Hawaii Protective Association, Ltd.)

Office of Hawaiian Affairs (Clayton Hee, Chair)

Graphic House, Inc.

KCCN Radio

International Life Support

Hawaiian Air

Aloha Airlines

Dr. Michael Chun & Kamehameha Schools/Bishop Estate

St. Andrew's Cathedral

Dwight Yoshimura, Pres., Ala Moana Center

Hoʻalikū Drake

Agnes Kalanihoʻokaha Cope

Bank of Hawaiʻi

Estate of James Campbell

Musicians' Association of Hawaiʻi Local 677

Bertrand & Beatrice Block

Kost A. Pankiwskyj

Rick/Carolyn S. Pompilio

E. K. Fernandez

Hawaiian Business/Professional Association

William E. Pimental

Island Insurance Company, Ltd.

R. J. Pfeiffer

Gentry Hawaiʻi, Ltd.

Finance Enterprises PAC

Uejo & Yamamoto, DDS, Inc.

Hawaiʻi National Bank

Hawaiʻi Hotel Industry Foundation

Susan E. Miller

Oceanic Cablevision

Council of Hawaiian Organizations, Inc.

Otaka, Inc. (Yukio Takahashi)

Jane E. Campbell

IBEW Local 1186

United Brotherhood of Carpenters & Joiners

Hawaiʻi Teamsters & Allied Workers' Union

Windward Worship Center

Rene Mansho, Councilmember City Council of Honolulu

Woody Barboza

Walter Akimo

Omar the Tent Man

NĀ KŌKUA MANAWALEʻA (ʻONIPAʻA VOLUNTEERS)

Nā Hui (Organizations):

Māmakakaua (Daughters & Sons
   of Hawaiian Warriors)
State Council on Hawaiian
   Heritage
ʻAhahui Kaʻahumanu
Hawaiʻi Teamsters - Local 996
Hawaiian Heritage Equestrians
Hawaiian Civic Club of Honolulu
Nā Pualei O Likolehua
Ka Lāhui Hawaiʻi

Hui Naʻauao
Office of Hawaiian Affairs (OHA)
Royal Order of Kamehameha
U.H. Office of the Vice-Pres.
   for University Relations
State Council of Hawaiian
   Homestead Associations
Pearl Harbor Hawaiian Civic Club
Hale O Nā Aliʻi
Pilikana O Koʻolauloa

Nā Kanaka (Individuals)

Anne Inouye
Stewart Ching
Aloha Silva
Alice Franco
Kimo Windrath
Dane Kiahe
Gladyce Clement
Harriet Seabury
Pualani Darby
Tina ʻAulani Wilhelm
Walter Akimo
Kauʻi Pratt
Regina Gregory
John Morris
ʻEhukaiolikoikamakani Hee
Marianne Lam
Reid Brown
Beverly Russell
Cynthia N. Ahn

Sharvani McBee
Darla Neves
David Munroe
Donald Bishaw
Oliver Ahmow
Lynn Chong-Albert
Peggy Goaney
Abigail Rosa
Annette Wilhelm
Max Wilhelm
Irene Takata
Paulette Silva
Pamela Jayne
Hoʻōulunonālani Hee
Peggy Lee
Hisao Yamashita
Edwin Quinabo
Corbit K. Ahn

List of Honolulu Police Department Officers who worked during the week of January 10th through the 17th

Chief Michael Nakamura
Major Bossie Correa
Lt. Alfredo Torco
Sgt. Cliff Kāneʻaiakalā
Officer Kenneth Creekmur
Officer Donald Marumoto
Officer Melvin Nākanelua
Officer Donald Nielson
Officer Milton Andrade
Officer Henry Ah Loo
Officer Kenneth Higa
Officer Dennis Ono
Officer Moana Heu
Officer Robert Trela
Officer Kaipo Miller
Officer Guy Nāhale

Asst. Chief Joseph Aveiro
Capt. Henry Robinson
Sgt. Derek Shimatsu
Sgt. Clay Cockett
Officer Allan Silva
Officer Peter Tampon
Officer Bryant Bayne
Officer Roy Fuata
Officer Foster Afalava
Officer Lew Kaeo
Officer Ted Honda
Officer Philip Trani
Officer Tommy Toyozaki
Officer Ken Miyazaki
Officer Clyde Kalepolo
Officer Keith Pimenta

Street Drama Volunteers (Actors)

Leo Anderson Akana
Kalani Akana
   & students/Waiau Elem.
Leinaʻala Naipo Akamine
Alani Apio
Kiʻilei Balaz
Lyla Berg
Bennett Berman
Stephen Boggs
Boyd Bond
Burl Burlingame
Jim Campbell
Kale Cheek
Montie Derby
Kioni Dudley
Elizabeth Nālani Ellis
David Eyre
Ernie Figueroa
Harry Fisher
Kaiopua Fyfe
Glen Grant
Matthew Gorton
Stephen Hancock
Kevin Hands
Louis Hao

Leināʻala Kalama Heine
Darren Hochstedler
Tom Hopcroft
Jonah Hulbert
Neil Hulbert
Ilona Ireijo
Kathe James
Charles Kaʻaiʻai
Sabra Kauka McCracken
Vai Keola
Bruss Keppeler
Jack Keppeler
Victoria Nalani Kneubuhl
Tory Laitila
Karen Loebl
Alexis Lopez
Anela Lopez
Bill Ogilvie
Nalani Olds
Marcus Oshiro
David Martin
Alika Maunakea
Buck Mickelson
Kīhei Soli Nīheu
Kūnani Nihipali

Frank Nobriga
Paul Sakimoto
Niklaus Schweitzer
Eric Seabury
Joseph Serrao
Leonard Stolfi, Jr.
Dallas Mossman Vogeler
Stephen Vogeler
Samuel Zap
Royal Order of
   Kamehameha
Royal Guard/Hawaiʻi
   National Guard

Table of Contents

January 17 . . .

ʻONIPAʻA
BOOK COMMITTEE

James Bartels, Elizabeth Pa Martin, Melvin Kalāhiki, Senator Eloise Ululani Tungpalan, Palani Vaughan and Betty Lou Stroup. Not pictured Robb Loo. (Russell Ho photo)

FOREWORD
SENATOR ELOISE ULULANI TUNGPALAN
'ONIPA'A CENTENNIAL COMMITTEE CHAIR

On behalf of the 'Onipa'a Centennial Committee, it gives me great pleasure to present this book as a lasting memento of one of the most important commemorative events ever held in our state. 'Onipa'a, to be steadfast, determined and resolute, was the motto of Hawai'i's last reigning monarch, Queen Lili'uokalani. The Centennial Committee, which coordinated the five days of events in observance of the January 17, 1893 overthrow of the Hawaiian monarchy, offers this book as a legacy of truth and understanding for everyone.

In April of 1992, the Hawai'i State Legislature and the Office of Hawaiian Affairs appropriated funds to commemorate the 100th anniversary of the overthrow of the Hawaiian monarchy. The 'Onipa'a Centennial Committee was then appointed by the Office of Hawaiian Affairs to coordinate and oversee the centennial activities. It was the hope of the Legislature, OHA, and the Centennial Committee that the observance of these activities would recall the events which led to the overthrow of the Hawaiian kingdom, then allow for a period of peaceful reflection. The culmination of this commemoration would be a firm resolution to address the long-standing concerns of the Hawaiian people. It was further hoped that this occasion would serve as a unifying event for the Hawaiian community and a significant step on the road to self-determination.

The 'Onipa'a Centennial Committee feels that the success of the commemorative events was evidenced by the participation of tens of thousands of people gathering to honor Queen Lili'uokalani in the spirit of pride, peace, dignity and unity. As the indigenous people, Hawaiians carry with them the deepest historical connection to the Hawaiian islands. This remarkable event allowed the Hawaiian people to collectively share the burdens of the past one hundred years. It also provided an opportunity for non-Hawaiians to understand and share that burden.

Our community has become far richer because of 'Onipa'a. We have seen that the obstacles of the past are surmountable and that by working together we can resolve differences and current problems. If we continue to make room for others in our thoughts and actions, all things are possible.

The preservation of Hawaiian culture and the Hawaiian race is a task that will require everyone's help. The 'Onipa'a Centennial Committee created this book in order to have a permanent record of this momentous and historic occasion. We hope that this publication may serve as a keepsake for all who wish to remember our beloved heritage and race. In so doing, we will be laying a firm foundation of peace for ourselves and for all future generations.

Mahalo Nui Loa,

Eloise U. Tungpalan

Eloise Ululani Tungpalan, Senator
Hawai'i State Legislature

OFFICE OF HAWAIIAN AFFAIRS

XVI

MEMBERS OF THE BOARD
Clayton H. W. Hee
    Trustee, O'ahu
    Chair, Board of Trustees
Abraham Aiona
    Trustee, Maui
    Vice Chair, Board of Trustees
    Chair, Committee on Budget, Finance and Policy
Moanike'ala Akaka
    Trustee, Hawai'i
    Chair, Committee on Human Services
Rowena Noelani Akana
    Trustee-at-Large
A. Frenchy Keānuenueokalaninuiamamao De Soto
    Trustee-at-Large
    Chair, Committee on Legislative Review
Kīna'u Boyd Kamali'i
    Trustee-at-Large
    Chair, Committee on Land and Sovereignty
Kamaki A. Kanahele III
    Trustee-at-Large
    Chair, Committee on Education and Culture
Moses Kapalekilahao Keale, Sr.
    Trustee, Kaua'i and Ni'ihau
    Chair, Committee on Planning, Economic
        Development and Housing
Samuel Lyons Kealoha, Jr.
    Trustee, Moloka'i and Lāna'i

PREFACE
CLAYTON HEE
CHAIRMAN, OFFICE OF HAWAIIAN AFFAIRS

'Ano'ai me ke aloha,

One hundred years have passed since the Kingdom of Hawai'i was illegally overthrown. One hundred years have passed since the first calls for justice were sounded, and left to echo unanswered. One hundred years — five generations waiting for the pain to end and the healing to begin; generations dying as justice is delayed.

As we observe the centennial of the illegal overthrow of Queen Lili'uokalani, let us note but not dwell on the long wait for justice. Rather, let us focus on the opportunities available to achieve ultimate justice for *nā kānaka*, the Hawaiian people.

We know the State of Hawai'i is seeking to strengthen the two public land trusts created for the benefit of native Hawaiians. We stand committed to the full repair of these two trusts administered by the Department of Hawaiian Home Lands and the Office of Hawaiian Affairs. But there can be no confusion about these trusts being compensation for the illegal overthrow. These trusts are separate and distinct from the settlement of claims arising out of the overthrow.

We hold that the state government is able and must contribute to the resolution of harms resulting from the illegal overthrow. But we know that it is the federal government which has the greater duty and power to settle Native Hawaiian land claims and to recognize the inherent right of Native Hawaiians to self-determined governance.

We also know neither the state nor the federal government will exercise those powers unless the cause of justice for Hawaiians is pursued not only by Hawaiians, but by all the citizens of Hawai'i to right what has been wrong for too long. Only then, united in cause and purpose, can *nā kānaka* realistically look to the federal and state governments for a comprehensive and long overdue settlement of claims for land and self-government.

The Office of Hawaiian Affairs has designated the 1990s as "The Decade of Decision." We are confident the power of the Centennial to inspire understanding and to inform action will take our cause for justice from these islands to the Congress and to the White House.

We must end this "Century of Dishonor"; we must end the mourning for a stolen nation. Instead, we must finally begin to honor the true legacy of Queen Lili'uokalani — *'Onipa'a* — to be steadfast in building a new Hawaiian nation founded on democratic principles and sustained by an equitable restoration of land and rights to the Hawaiian people. We can. We must.

E lanakila kākou. I ho'okahi pu'uwai me ka lōkahi.

Let us move forward with one heart strengthened by unity.

'O au nō me ka ha'aha'a,

Clayton H. W. Hee, Chairman
Board of Trustees

ACKNOWLEDGMENTS

The 'Onipa'a Centennial Committee was privileged to have had the opportunity to plan and coordinate the events marking the 100th anniversary of the overthrow of the kingdom of Queen Lili'uokalani. Thousands of people gathered to watch and participate in the five days of centennial activities. Many were unable to be present, so the idea of sharing this momentous time through a pictorial document was discussed and agreed upon by the 'Onipa'a Centennial Committee.

To fully acknowledge all who have given so generously of their time and energy to make this book a reality is an impossible task. Words of gratitude will never be able to express our entire feelings of appreciation to the members of the 'Onipa'a Book Committee: Chair Elizabeth Pa Martin, past president of Hui Na'auao and director of the Native Hawaiian Advisory Council; Palani Vaughan, senior assistant in the state Office of International Relations of the Office of the Governor; Betty Lou Stroup and James Bartels of The Friends of 'Iolani Palace; Robb Loo, United Airlines flight attendant; Melvin Kalāhiki, senior president of the Council of Hawaiian Organizations; and 'Onipa'a Chair, State Senator Eloise Tungpalan. Their commitment to accurately document the 'Onipa'a story has made it possible for everyone to enjoy this legacy today.

We also wish to extend our deepest gratitude to the families of the Book Committee members. There were many sacrifices and adjustments made by their families in an effort to support the work of the committee. We wish to say "*Mahalo nui loa*" to all!

The 'Onipa'a Committee is sincerely grateful to the trustees of the Office of Hawaiian Affairs. Their financial support made it possible to create this book, and a statement of "*Mahalo nui loa*" can only begin to record our feelings of *aloha* for them.

We would not have gone very far without the services of the capable staff at the Office of Hawaiian Affairs: Government Affairs Officer Scotty Bowman; Apolei Bargamento and the late Andrea Akana; and Peggy Lee of Senator Tungpalan's office.

We are especially indebted to the many photographers who so willingly shared their photos with the committee. They are Douglas Peebles, Eileen Kalāhiki, Holly Henderson, Verna Kong, Annelore Niejahr, Kai Joger, K. Russell Ho, Lani Ma'a Lapilio, JHC, Robb Loo, The Friends of 'Iolani Palace, Elizabeth Pa Martin, Joseph Chang, Ken Sakamoto, David Shapiro, Bruce Asato, Carl Viti, Gregory Yamamoto, Take Umeda, Deborah Booker, Deborah Ward, Jeff Clark, and David Yamada.

A great appreciative *aloha* to *Honolulu Advertiser* editor Gerry Keir, editorial page editor Jerry Burris and chief photographer David Yamada for their invaluable services in lending photos taken during 'Onipa'a to our committee. We also wish to acknowledge *Honolulu Advertiser* reporter Stu Glauberman, whose historical account of the overthrow is reprinted in this work with his permission.

Our warmest *mahalo* to *Honolulu Star-Bulletin* editor and publisher John Flanagan, photo editor Ken Sakamoto, and the many *Star-Bulletin* photographers who greatly assisted us with 'Onipa'a photos printed in the *Star-Bulletin.* A special *mahalo* to receptionist Judy Amancio for her assistance in providing the *Star-Bulletin* photos.

We are sincerely thankful to all the donors who supported 'Onipa'a. A list of their names and organizations is presented in this book. Their faith in our program will always be remembered.

We are very thankful to the Honorable John Waihe'e, Governor of the State of Hawai'i, and the Honorable Frank F. Fasi, Mayor of the City and County of Honolulu, for their invaluable assistance and *aloha* throughout the planning and implementation phases of the centennial observances.

We are most appreciative of the Hawai'i State Legislature and the Office of Hawaiian Affairs for their joint funding of the 'Onipa'a centennial events.

Our most heartfelt *aloha* to William Paty, the diligent and patient past Chairman of the Department of Land and Natural Resources, and his capable staff of Mahi Pekelo and Ralston Nagata, who enabled the 'Onipa'a Committee to bring together the many diverse groups who participated in the centennial activities.

Mahalo nui loa to State Director of Accounting and General Services Robert Takushi and Honolulu City Council Chair Gary Gill for providing parking spaces for centennial participants.

The skills and training of Sgt. Cliff Kāne'aiakalā and the competence of the Honolulu Police Department's officers who were assigned to keep the peace were much appreciated by all.

Our warmest *aloha* and *mahalo* to all the people and organizations who participated and observed with peace and dignity throughout the entire centennial events. You were great!

To our speedy word processors, Tina Roberts, Jimmy Chan and Adam Gould, we thank you for the many sleepless nights it took to finish this project.

Many thanks to writer Victoria Kneubuhl, designer Michael Horton, and publisher Bennett Hymer for their kind patience and assistance as we worked feverishly to meet our book deadlines. A warm *mahalo* to Glen Grant for his *kōkua* in skillfully weaving our stories into this book. James Bartels, curator of the Friends of 'Iolani Palace, devoted many hours to editing the manuscript.

To Cobey Black and Momi Lum, we wish to extend our sincerest *aloha* for reviewing and editing our work and encouraging us to persevere in completing this book.

Finally, a heartfelt gratitude to all the members of the 'Onipa'a Centennial Committee! Your efforts produced a memorable five days of activities which provided the foundation for this book.

'Onipa'a kākou!

Eloise U. Tungpalan

Eloise Ululani Tungpalan, Chair
'Onipa'a Centennial Committee

INTRODUCTION
JOHN D. WAIHE'E III
GOVERNOR, STATE OF HAWAI'I

".....until such time as the Government of the United States shall, upon the facts being presented to it, undo the action of its representatives and reinstate me in the authority which I claim as the constitutional sovereign of the Hawaiian Islands."
—Queen Lili'uokalani, 1893

When Queen Lili'uokalani, relinquished, under protest, her authority to the newly formed provisional government of Hawai'i in 1893, little did she imagine the length of time it would take the Government of the United States to recognize their complicity in the overthrow. Little did she imagine how long it would take for that government to offer a formal apology. And little did she dream that the reinstatement of her sovereign nation would still not be achieved more than 100 years later.

That is the unvarnished truth of where contemporary Native Hawaiians find themselves. Words such as "overdue justice," "long-standing grievances," and "long-suffering" are all applicable to our history and our plight, but, they are not the only words. "Pride," "resilience," and "determination" are others.

Not since the overthrow have Native Hawaiians been closer to reinstating sovereignty than today. There are cynics who scoff at that assessment, who say it will never happen unless other seemingly difficult conditions are resolved first — because Hawaiians themselves are too divided, because the State is too intrusive, because other groups in Hawai'i will not allow it, because .....

I, obviously, do not agree with these naysayers. I believe in the spirit and determination of the Hawaiian people, and I believe in the collective wisdom and *aloha* of all the people of Hawai'i. I believe in the rightness of our cause and the system of justice in this country which, having failed Native Hawaiians 100 years ago, has the ability and obligation to right those wrongs.

And, I believe there are many Hawaiians today who, in the words of the Queen, are truly not afraid to act for fear of failing and who are willing to do the hard work to correct a grievous wrong. The 'Onipa'a Centennial Observance marks the hundredth year of our struggle, as well as a rebirth and rededication of our commitment to see it to its rightful end.

JOHN D. WAIHE'E III
Governor, State of Hawai'i

'ONIPA'A

A Prologue to
Five Days in the
History of the Hawaiian Nation

'Onipa'a: Five Days in the History of the Hawaiian Nation is the story of how two five-day periods in January separated by a century were linked by an extraordinary spiritual, cultural and political steadfastness. It is the chronicle of an outpouring of devotion to a determined Queen whose call for the restitution of justice for her people has not yet been answered. The story is told in thousands of small kaleidoscopic pieces — of numerous Native Hawaiian organizations and individuals linking arms to express their common concerns in a myriad of ways, private and public leaders sharing their sentiments and visions, costumed theatrical role-players re-enacting the past so as to promote a vivid understanding of what took place in history.

For the many non-Hawaiians who attended the 'Onipa'a events, this was a time of listening to the voice of Hawai'i's indigenous people spoken from podiums, informally shared by folks sitting on nearby mats or often simply revealed in their tear-soaked eyes. The most important stories were being told in the hundreds of clusters of friends and family who gathered day after day, from early morning through the evening with their *kūpuna* and children, to experience the sights and sounds of history and to uncover their feelings of what it means to be a Hawaiian at the close of the twentieth century.

Throughout these five days of events it was readily apparent that their devotion to a determined Queen was steadfast. Hawaiians and non-Hawaiians united as Hawai'i's people to share in this historic, spiritual and cultural observance. The extraordinary solemnity, dignity and spirituality of the observance culminated in front of 'Iolani Palace as Queen Lili'uokalani's words were about to be delivered by Leo Anderson Akana from the steps of 'Iolani Palace as thousands of Hawaii's people gathered on the Palace grounds, once the setting for the coronation of King Kalākaua in 1883. The mood this day, however, was somber, the audience subdued and anxious. The faces of the *kūpuna,* the elders, were sometimes marked with tears that, after so many years, now flowed freely for the loss of

their nation. Anger and disappointment were not absent from those gathered to hear the words of the Queen, but a bond of healing had transformed their rage into a common commitment to the sovereignty of a nation. Schoolchildren and toddlers, families and office workers, *kama'āina* from all the Hawaiian islands from Hawai'i to Ni'ihau, Native Hawaiian homesteaders and urban apartment dwellers, taro farmers and truck drivers, dignitaries and common folk, all distinctions erased save for common heritage, silently waited on a January day under the white warmth of a tropical sun.

"My people" were the words the Queen had used to address her loyal subjects on the afternoon of Saturday, January 14, 1893. A stillness pervaded the air as those words were now spoken for the gathered assembly. How long had it been since the Native Hawaiian nation had heard those words once legitimately used by one of their *ali'i?* The Queen's speech explained how the promulgation of a new constitution, which would restore the rights of the monarchy while protecting the voting rights of the people, had been prevented. To avoid violence in her politically volatile kingdom, her people were urged to return to their homes to await the day when she would be able to grant them the document that would preserve their rights and freedom. Her words were ennobling and dignified, reminding those assembled that the love of nation and the common bond of ancestry are inalienable.

As the Queen's words concluded, an uncanny feeling permeated the crowd: that the distance of 100 years of pain and loss separating several generations had just vanished. Had not a similar crowd of loyal subjects stood at this same place in 1893, caught up in the historic chain of events that would within three days destroy a nation? For the thousands of Hawai'i's people gathered in 1993, the knowledge that history cannot be reversed only strengthened their resolve. These historic days 100 years later were to be not only for remembrance and mourning; but also for the healing of the wounds of the past and a rebirth of a Hawaiian nation.

2

'ONIPA'A
FIVE DAYS
IN THE
HISTORY
OF THE
HAWAIIAN
NATION

1893-1993

The Hawaiian Nation: Past and Present

CHAPTER ONE

The Hawaiian Monarchy
Preserving the Life of the Land

The Hawaiian nation reaches back into antiquity, when history was recorded in *oli,* chant, and the land was deified by *akua,* the gods and *'aumākua,* family ancestors. Among the native people, the leadership of society was in the hands of the *ali'i* or chiefs who, as stewards of the land, were responsible for the spiritual and physical well-being of the *maka'āinana,* the people. Through the counsel of *kāhuna,* teachers and priests, the *ali'i* ruled from time immemorial.

With the Hawaiian islands' entry into the international struggle between Western empires in the late eighteenth century, the *ali'i* became increasingly aware that the independence of their nation required a precarious strategy which balanced the interests of mercantile powers seeking to expand their influence throughout the Pacific and Asia. As long as all foreign powers wanted a special foothold in Hawai'i, no single nation would dare usurp the tiny kingdom's sovereignty. Situated at a crossroads of the Pacific Ocean, the Hawaiian islands became, as Native Hawaiian historian David Malo warned, the "little fish" pursued by the "big fish."

The Hawaiian nation which had been unified under Kamehameha I in 1810 sought international alliances which would perpetuate the rule of the native people under their chiefs. Even the flag of the Hawaiian kingdom symbolized in its pattern and colors the intention of this Polynesian nation to be friends to all countries, possessed by none. As American economic, cultural, and military interests in the islands grew throughout the nineteenth century, the stage was being set for a confrontation leading to the overthrow of the Hawaiian monarchy and the dispossession of the *kānaka maoli.* A century later, the Native Hawaiians remember their monarchs with reverence, recognizing the struggles of their chiefs to chart a wise path through the turbulent storms of disease, upheaval and change that swept the islands of Hawai'i.

'ONIPA'A
FIVE DAYS
IN THE
HISTORY
OF THE
HAWAIIAN
NATION

1893-1993

(Hawai'i State Archives photo)

KAMEHAMEHA I

Reign: 1795-1819

Kamehameha I was born in Kohala on the island of Hawai'i around 1758. Trained as a powerful warrior, by 1795 he brought the islands of Hawai'i, Maui, Moloka'i, Lāna'i and O'ahu under his control through military conquest. Many foreigners who had arrived in Hawai'i during this time encouraged rivalry among the ruling chiefs by selling guns and ammunition to both sides. Desiring to create a unified nation, Kamehameha struggled to bring Kaua'i under his control. Finally, in 1810, Kaumuali'i, the ruling chief of Kaua'i, recognized the supreme authority of Kamehameha. The Kingdom of Hawai'i had been established and the Kamehameha dynasty began a 62-year rule. Though Kamehameha maintained most native traditions and customs during his reign, foreign influence continued to grow as the sandalwood trade linked Hawai'i to the Canton trade routes. When this great chief died in 1819, the question arose whether Kamehameha's son and his councilors would be able to hold the nation together in the face of the undermining of ancient traditional ways and beliefs, and the mounting death rates from introduced foreign diseases.

6

'ONIPA'A
FIVE DAYS
IN THE
HISTORY
OF THE
HAWAIIAN
NATION

1893-1993

TAMEHAMEHA 2.º
HIS MAJESTY THE KING OF THE
SANDWICH ISLANDS.
[By Authority] Drawn on Stone from Life by John Hayter.
London Pub.ª by R. Ackermann, Nº 191, Strand, June 1824.

(Hawai'i State Archives photo)

KAMEHAMEHA II

Reign: 1819-1824

'Iolani Liholiho was born in 1797 to Kamehameha I and Keōpūolani. Raised during long years of peace, Liholiho succeeded his father as Kamehameha II at age 22 with no experience in commanding troops, fighting battles or ruling an island. He shared his power with the *kuhina nui,* Ka'ahumanu, the politically influential widow of his father.

Ka'ahumanu and the Council of Chiefs pressured Liholiho to abolish the chiefly state religion and *kapu* system. By taking this politically expedient course of action, they would weaken the power and prestige of rival chiefs and also minimize conflicts between traditional customs and new Western practices. Consequently, in 1819 Liholiho ordered the destruction of *heiau* and religious idols and thereby ended the chiefly state religion and the *kapu* system. This system of sacred prohibitions and restrictions had been the only law in the nation for many centuries — from that time forward, the laws would be ordained directly by the monarch.

The brief reign of Kamehameha II coincided with an increased western presence in the islands as foreign sandalwood merchants settled in ports such as Honolulu and were followed by a growing whaling industry. The first American Protestant missionaries landed at Kawaihae, Hawai'i, in 1820 and soon established their stations in Kailua-Kona, Honolulu, Lahaina and Waimea, Kaua'i. As the foreign population grew, the Hawaiian population declined drastically to 135,000 by 1823. By way of contrast, population estimates for 1778, the year of Captain Cook's arrival, ranged from a low of 400,000 to a high of 800,000. By either measure, the native population was perishing as a generation of Christianized chiefs attempted to stabilize the society through education, churches and new laws derived from the Ten Commandments. During a trip to Great Britain to visit King George IV, Kamehameha II and his wife Kamāmalu died in London in 1824 after contracting measles. The fate of the Hawaiian Throne was left in the hands of his younger brother, Kauikeaouli.

KAMEHAMEHA III

Reign: 1825-1854

(Hawai'i State Archives photo)

Kauikeaouli succeeded to the throne as Kamehameha III in 1825 when he was only 12 years old. Ka'ahumanu continued as regent and Kalanimoku, a high ranking chief, served as the king's special guardian. Missionaries taught Kauikeaouli the Christian religion, writing and reading. He proclaimed the Declaration of Rights, known as the Hawaiian Magna Carta, in 1839, and in 1840 promulgated the first constitution for the kingdom. He divided the land of Hawai'i among the king, government, *ali'i* and people through the Mahele in 1848 and the Kuleana Act of 1850. Foreigners were allowed to become naturalized citizens in 1845 and to own land in 1850.

In February 1843, the sovereignty of Hawai'i was taken away by the British for six months. On July 31, 1843, British Admiral Thomas restored Hawai'i's sovereignty. During the restoration ceremonies, Kamehameha III spoke the words, "*Ua mau ke ea o ka 'āina i ka pono*" (The life of the land is preserved in righteousness).

The constitution of 1852 replaced the first constitution during Kauikeaouli's reign. Kamehameha III ruled the Hawaiian islands longer than any other monarch, and the years of his reign were marked by significant legal changes that transformed the relationship of the chiefs and people. Although the door had been opened to foreigners obtaining land, the king had established a legislature where representatives determined the law and extended democratic voting rights to his subjects.

At the time of Kamehameha III's death in 1854, a constitutional monarchy had been firmly established in the Hawaiian islands based upon the enfranchisement of a highly literate native population. This Polynesian nation negotiated treaties with foreign nations, exchanged consuls, and fully recognized how precious was national independence.

7

FIVE DAYS
IN THE
HISTORY
OF THE
HAWAIIAN
NATION

8

'ONIPA'A
FIVE DAYS
IN THE
HISTORY
OF THE
HAWAIIAN
NATION

1893-1993

(Hawai'i State Archives photo)

KAMEHAMEHA IV

Reign: 1854 - 1863

Before his death in 1854, Kamehameha III selected his nephew Alexander Liholiho, the grandson of Kamehameha I, as heir apparent. Educated in the Chiefs' Children School, or Royal School, as a young man Alexander Liholiho had traveled with his brother to the United States, where he experienced first hand the racial prejudice that had segregated African-Americans. The young princes of Hawai'i had been questioned due to their dark complexions when they attempted to board a Washington, D.C. trolley. Determined to stop the encroaching influences of American sugar planters and merchants in the islands, Kamehameha IV favored the monarchical style and Anglican faith of Great Britain. During his reign, he was also determined to deal with the continuing public health crisis brought about by the ravaging effects of foreign diseases. With the aid of Queen Emma, his wife, he established the Queen's Hospital in 1859. He also introduced modern protocol and etiquette to his court, modeling it after those in Europe. Although Kamehameha IV and Queen Emma had produced an heir to the Hawaiian throne, young Prince Albert Leiopapa-a-Kamehameha died tragically at the age of four. The young king died 18 months later at the age of 29, his resolute independent leadership earning for him the enduring affection of his people.

(Hawaiʻi State Archives photo)

KAMEHAMEHA V

Reign: 1863 - 1872

Lot Kapuāiwa succeeded his brother to the throne, and proved himself a faithful guardian of Hawaiian sovereignty. He resisted the granting of concessions to foreign nations and returned to the Hawaiian crown many of the powers which it had previously possessed. Through his efforts, the third constitution of Hawaiʻi was established in 1864. It increased the powers of the monarch by freeing him of control by the privy council and the *kuhina nui*; it also set property qualifications for voting.

Sugar production grew exponentially in the islands during the 1860's with substantial American investment and Kamehameha V became increasingly suspicious of foreign designs on Hawaiʻi.

When the last of the ruling Kamehamehas died in 1872 without an heir apparent, he left behind many public works, including the new Aliʻiōlani Hale government building, the post office on Merchant Street, and the Opera House. Although a band had been part of the Hawaiian court under various names and leaders since 1815, Kamehameha V also revitalized the Royal Hawaiian Band under the leadership of Henri Berger, a German immigrant. Kamehameha V had also promoted a spirit of nationalism. In the coming decade it would fire the hearts of the native people with a new vision of pride, preservation and sovereignty.

FIVE DAYS
IN THE
HISTORY
OF THE
HAWAIIAN
NATION

(Hawai'i State Archives photo)

'ONIPA'A
FIVE DAYS
IN THE
HISTORY
OF THE
HAWAIIAN
NATION

1893-1993

LUNALILO

Reign: 1873 - 1874

William Charles Lunalilo, a grandson of Kamehameha's half brother, was the first elected king. Known as the "People's King" because of his popularity with Hawaiians, he reigned for only 13 months before dying of tuberculosis. Lunalilo effected amendments liberalizing the constitution of 1864, most notably the abolition of property qualifications for voting. He also founded the Lunalilo Home for indigent aged and infirmed Hawaiians. Since Lunalilo had named no heir apparent to the throne, upon his death, the House of Nobles was once again called upon to elect a king.

(Hawaiʻi State Archives photo)

KALĀKAUA

Reign: 1874 - 1891

David Laʻamea Kalākaua was elected monarch over Queen Emma, the widow of Kamehameha IV. During his reign, Kalākaua led a Hawaiian national renaissance, a revival of traditions including the performance of the *hula* (which had been suppressed through missionary influence), chants, sports and medicinal practices. With the motto *Hoʻoūlu Lāhui*, "increase the race," His Majesty Kalākaua attempted to reverse the continuing decline of the native population by restoring a sense of national pride. With Henri Berger, the conductor of the Royal Hawaiian Band, Kalākaua composed *Hawaiʻi Ponoʻī*, the stirring national anthem. He commissioned the building of ʻIolani Palace and the statue of Kamehameha I to elevate the prestige and influence of the monarchy. His coronation in 1883 was the shining capstone of his effort to stem the rising tide of foreign influences that threatened native control of the government. Yet as American capital dominated Hawaiʻi's economy during the 1880's and tens of thousands of Japanese laborers immigrated to work on the expanding sugar plantations, the prominence of Native Hawaiians in island society waned. Threatened by His Majesty's persistent nationalism, in 1887, a group of armed non-Hawaiian residents and businessmen forced Kalākaua to sign the Bayonet Constitution. This constitution restricted the voting rights of the Hawaiian people and severely limited the powers of the king. With the native population curtailed in influence, the political life of the islands became increasingly volatile. Then, in January 1891 Kalākaua died in San Francisco during a trip to the United States.

11

FIVE DAYS
IN THE
HISTORY
OF THE
HAWAIIAN
NATION

LILI‘UOKALANI

Reign: 1891- 1893

Queen Lili‘uokalani, the last reigning Hawaiian monarch, was King Kalākaua's younger sister and designated heir to the throne. Her personal motto was *‘Onipa‘a*, to remain steadfast. When she ascended the throne on her brother's death, she made public her opposition to the Bayonet Constitution of 1887 because it limited the rights of both the monarchs and Native Hawaiians. Considering her a threat to their business interests, a group of men, primarily American business-men, began to plot her over-throw through the establishment of the Annexation Club and through discussions with American diplomatic and naval representatives in the islands.

Amid this charged atmos-phere of political intrigue, Queen Lili‘uokalani steadfastly pursued efforts to rectify the injustices of the Bayonet Constitution through the promulgation of a new constitu-tion. The 1892 Legislature of the Kingdom of Hawai‘i failed, however, to endorse the convening of a constitutional convention. Petitions were circulating in the native commu-nities supporting the establish-ment of a new constitution, which would strengthen the position of the mon-arch while eliminating property qualifications on voting. The Queen moved to respond to the voice of her people. Her intention was to announce to the nation the promulgation of a new constitution on Saturday, January 14, 1893. In the tradition of

12

‘ONIPA‘A
FIVE DAYS
IN THE
HISTORY
OF THE
HAWAIIAN
NATION

1893-1993

Queen Lili‘uokalani retired to Washington Place where she would remain in quiet seclusion until her death on November 11, 1917. Her dignity and moral strength had not diminished as her call for justice to the United States government remained unanswered. One hundred years later the Hawaiian people still wait for the restoration of their sovereign nation. (Hawai‘i State Archives photo)

Hawaiian monarchs dating back to Kamehameha III, the legality of this change in government would be established by her signature. Her native subjects traveled to O‘ahu from all the islands, anticipating the restoration of the rights previously guaranteed them.

CHAPTER TWO

ʻŌNIPAʻA
Preparing to Encounter History

Reflecting upon the centennial of the January 17, 1893 overthrow of Queen Liliʻuokalani, as well as the culmination of the International Year of the World's Indigenous Peoples, there is no question that the cry for justice for Native Hawaiians continues to grow — in Hawaiʻi, across the country and throughout the world community.

Key to this endeavor will be the continued commitment of individuals, grass roots organizations, local and national policymakers, and international interests dedicated to our ongoing educational efforts regarding the issue of Hawaiian sovereignty and history surrounding the 1893 overthrow and its ramifications.

One thing is clear. No one person or group should chart the destiny of the Native Hawaiian people. As Native Hawaiians seek to determine their political goals, it is my sincere hope that geographical barriers and diverging views do not hinder our common pursuit of justice.

To assist our cause, I have called for a United Nations proclamation declaring an International Decade of the World's Indigenous Peoples and the establishment of international standards of our fundamental rights. It is my wholehearted belief that the future of Native Hawaiians is not merely a Native Hawaiian issue. It is a state issue. It is a national issue. It is a global issue.

There is no conflict between standing firm and being open to others. Our solidarity is only enhanced through our welcoming of every new believer in our crusade — and every new believer brings us that much closer to justice for the Native Hawaiian people and a better world for all.

Daniel K. Akaka
Senator, U.S. Congress

F or many decades, Hawaiians were only partially educated to the actual events of 1893 and the overthrow of their monarchy. As is often the case in history, the winners rewrite the past to serve their own needs, hoping through collective myth to obliterate memory. In classroom textbooks, the story of the overthrow was presented as "historical inevitability," the "triumph of democracy over feudalism," or simply the sad and regrettable consequence of the "passing of a race."

The pride of a nation, however, could not be extinguished. Many sources and voices awoke the descendants of *Papa* and *Wākea* from years of hurt, denial or amnesia to rediscover their own heritage. In song, dance, and prayer their teachers opened their eyes to *nā mea kahiko*, the things of old. In the political arena, a renewed sense of activism heightened their commitment to social change for the improvement of their native communities. Through the words of their ancestors, passed through oral tradition or in written form, the nation sought to face the events of 100 years ago, to understand the truth and to redefine the future.

As the 100th anniversary of the overthrow of the Hawaiian monarchy approached, scores of Hawaiian groups throughout the islands recognized that this was not only a time to reflect on the past. It was an opportunity to coalesce over 200,000 Hawaiian people and their non-Hawaiian supporters in a process of coming together for the purposes of education, healing and renewing a commitment to the concept of nation and sovereignty. In order to coordinate what would certainly be one of the most important public events in the lifetime of this generation of Hawaiians, the ʻOnipaʻa Centennial Committee was established by the Office of Hawaiian Affairs in 1992. The ʻOnipaʻa Centennial Committee members included Chairperson Senator Eloise Ululani Tungpalan, Vice Chair Francis McMillen, Rowena Akana, R-M. Keahi Allen, James Bartels, Peter Ching, Momi Cazimero, Dave Chun, Senator Mike Crozier, Rockne Freitas, Mufi Hannemann, Al Harrington, Wendy Roylo Hee, Leināʻala Heine, William Kaina, Melvin Kalāhiki, Kamaki A. Kanahele III, Edward Kaʻōpūʻiki, Keiji Kawakami, Lilinoe Lindsey, Elizabeth Pa Martin, Robert Pfeiffer, Wendell Silva, Margaret Kula Stafford, Betty Lou Stroup, Palani Vaughan, and Dallas Mossman Vogeler.

Central to the ʻOnipaʻa Centennial Committee's mission was the acknowledgment of the centennial of the illegal overthrow of Queen Liliʻuokalani and the Hawaiian sovereign nation. In re-enacting the historical events of the overthrow, the committee hoped to illustrate their significant and varied impact on the Hawaiian people. The objectives of the observance included celebrating the dedication Queen Liliʻuokalani displayed to her people, culture and heritage and providing inspiration to the Hawaiian people. Other endeavors sought to

ʻONIPAʻA
FIVE DAYS
IN THE
HISTORY
OF THE
HAWAIIAN
NATION

1893-1993

(Preceding page) Leo Akana Anderson, portraying Queen Liliʻuokalani stated: "My dear people of Hawaiʻi Nei, I have listened to the thousands of voices of my people that have come to me and I am prepared to grant their request. The present constitution is full of defects . . . I have prepared one in which the rights of all have been regarded, a constitution suited to the wishes of the dear people. . . " (*Advertiser* photo by T. Umeda) recognize the Queen's abilities as a brilliant composer, lyricist and writer and to emulate her spirituality, leadership, compassion and dignity. Ultimately, the committee strove to produce a centennial observance that would uphold Queen Liliʻuokalani's legacy which has sustained the Hawaiian people for 100 years.

The goal of the ʻOnipaʻa Centennial Committee was to facilitate the participation of all the people of Hawaiʻi who wished to join in observing the centennial of the overthrow of the monarchy. Every group or person who sought to express their feelings about the observance of this historical event would be included. The important task before the committee was to coordinate this massive effort with a spirit of openness and unity. Among the many

matters the committee had to consider was accommodating the large number of people wanting to participate in this event. Ensuring implementation of the many proposed events in an atmosphere of understanding and cooperation was paramount. Decisions addressed included fairness in involving the many different Hawaiian organizations in both the planning and programming, and fostering the cooperation of all agencies impacted by the commemoration.

Ambitious plans for a "living history" re-enactment of the last four days of the Hawaiian monarchy were also underway. Sponsored by the ʻOnipaʻa Centennial Committee and Hui Naʻauao, a diverse coalition of more than 40 Hawaiian organizations promoting education on Hawaiian self-

Concerns over the use of the Palace and grounds during the observances are worked out between state officials, ʻOnipaʻa Centennial Observance Committee members, Friends of ʻIolani Palace, and Hui Naʻauao including (*left to right*) Momi Cazimero, Charles Kaʻaiʻai, Melvin Kalāhiki, Palani Vaughan, Frank Nobriga, Michael Crozier, Leināʻala Heine, Chair Eloise Tungpalan, Donna Hanaike, Elizabeth Pa Martin, James Bartels, Betty Lou Stroup, Māhealani Kamauʻu, Edward Kaʻōpūiki, Ralston Nagata, William Paty and Dallas Vogeler. (Kai Joger photo)

determination, the pageant would dramatize historic events at the sites where they actually took place.

The idea for this program came from a proposal submitted by Dallas Mossman Vogeler and Charles Ka'ai'ai, who had enlisted the help of Victoria N. Kneubuhl as scriptwriter. A cast of over 100 costumed role-players spent six months rehearsing their roles, researching their characters, and preparing to step back in time. Efforts were made to obtain authentic costumes and props, even anticipating a re-creation of the January 16, 1893 illegal landing of United States military troops on Hawaiian soil.

Behind-the-scenes negotiations both before and during the observances included working closely with the Friends of 'Iolani Palace and the Department of Land and Natural Resources to utilize the grounds and Palace for several unique and symbolic purposes. The 'Onipa'a Committee met with representatives of the Friends of 'Iolani Palace and William Paty, Director of DLNR, to arrange for Leo Anderson Akana, the actress portraying Queen Lili'uokalani, to stand on the Palace steps and balcony during part of her "living history" performance. In addition, discussions were held to allow an *ahu* or stone shrine to be constructed upon the Palace grounds. The late Parley Kanaka'ole led a *ho'oponopono* between the Friends of 'Iolani Palace and Hawaiians interested in constructing the *ahu*. The *ahu* was meant to be a symbol of the intent to heal the pain between the *maka'-āinana* and the *ali'i.*

A primary planning concern was crowd safety. To promote a spirit of harmony throughout the observance, the committee asked participating groups to organize peace-keepers among their members. These peace-keepers would assist with equipment setup and the movement of actors, actresses and dignitaries through the large crowds to facilitate the constant ebb and flow of thousands of people.

The Honolulu Police Department, the state

First meeting of the 'Onipa'a Centennial Committee.
(*Advertiser* **photo by T. Umeda**)

18

'ONIPA'A
FIVE DAYS
IN THE
HISTORY
OF THE
HAWAIIAN
NATION

1893-1993

The peacekeepers receive training in nonviolent tactics to prepare for any possible disruption which could take place during the centennial activities.
(**Elizabeth Pa Martin photo**)

Department of Land and Natural Resources, the state Department of Parks and Recreation, the 'Ohana Council, Hui Na'auao, the Council of Hawaiian Organizations, Ka Lāhui Hawai'i, and other Hawaiian organizations coordinated security and logistics concerns. Several meetings were held between police officers and Hawaiian organizations so that everyone could share their *mana'o* on public safety, traffic control and other related matters. Arrangements were made to close King Street during some activities so as to facilitate marches and historical re-enactments. The positive attitude of Police Sergeant Clifford Kāne'aiakalā and the members of the Honolulu Police Department's Specialized Services Unit was greatly appreciated throughout the centennial events. Sergeant Kāne'aiakalā would later receive an award for the way he performed his duties during the 'Onipa'a centennial activities.

As all these preparations were taking place, one of the concerns of the 'Onipa'a Committee was the objectivity of the coverage which the dozens of anniversary events would receive from the local press. Prior to the opening ceremonies, 'Onipa'a Centennial Chair Eloise Ululani Tungpalan and committee members Momi Cazimero, Elizabeth Pa Martin, Wendy Roylo-Hee, R-M. Keahi Allen, Dallas Mossman Vogeler, Melvin Kalāhiki, and Palani Vaughan met first with John Flanagan, editor of the *Honolulu Star-Bulletin*, and then with editor Gerry Keir and reporter Stu Glauberman of *The Honolulu Advertiser*. After a candid exchange of concerns, 'Onipa'a Committee members left the Hawai'i Newspaper Agency building feeling reassured that both newspapers would give fair coverage to the centennial observance events.

Anticipation mounted throughout the islands as this critical moment in the history of the Hawaiian nation neared. On Saturday, January 9, the weekend before the opening of the 'Onipa'a centennial activities, the 'Ohana Council held a benefit concert at 'Iolani Palace that featured the talents of many island musicians, including Mākaha Sons of Ni'ihau, Jerry Santos, Haunani Apoliona and Wally Suyenaga. The concert set a positive tone while awakening the community's interest in the Hawaiian sovereignty issues that would be brought up in the

Jerry Santos, Haunani Apoliona and Wally Suyenaga entertain the large crowd attending the 'Ohana Council Benefit Concert on January 9 in front of 'Iolani Palace. (Elizabeth Pa Martin photo)

The 'Ohana Council Benefit Concert was broadcast live on KCCN radio. Kimo Kahōano (*right*) interviews Ernest Heen and OHA Trustee Moanike'ala Akaka during the program. (Elizabeth Pa Martin photo)

'Onipa'a Committee members meet with *Honolulu Advertiser* editor Gerry Keir and reporter Stu Glauberman. Pictured are (*left to right*) Wendy Roylo-Hee, Melvin Kalāhiki, Palani Vaughan, Stu Glauberman, Momi Cazimero, Eloise Ululani Tungpalan, Gerry Keir and Keahi Allen (*with her back to the camera*). (Elizabeth Pa Martin photo)

coming days.

Although many indigenous voices are attempting to define "sovereignty," these coming days would enhance their efforts toward mutual understanding and cooperation. As actors rehearsed their lines late into the night and behind-the-scenes coordinators took care of the final details, as Hawaiians from Maui, Hawai'i, Moloka'i, Kaua'i, Ni'ihau and Lāna'i caught late flights to O'ahu, a sobering sense of the spiritual importance of the activities to take place settled upon all those who had labored to make 'Onipa'a a reality.

At 9:30 on the morning of January 13, 1993, before the opening of official ceremonies, the 'Onipa'a Centennial Committee gathered at the Royal Mausoleum at Mauna 'Ala. This quiet spot nestled in Nu'uanu Valley has long been the resting place of Hawaiian *ali'i*. With the permission of Royal Mausoleum caretaker Lydia Nāmahana Maioho, the committee and their invited guests

came to this sacred place, in time-honored tradition, to ask the blessings of their ancestors. The Hawaiian concept of *'ohana* and community includes all living members of the Hawaiian race and those who have passed on. Important endeavors are blessed when the living honor the spirits of their ancestors.

As the group entered Mauna 'Ala Chapel, the voice of Wendell Ka-lani-kapu-'ae-nui Silva chanted an ancient *oli*. Once inside, 'Onipa'a Chair Eloise Ululani Tungpalan expressed the committee's *aloha* for Queen Lili'uokalani and asked for her blessings on the observance. From the chapel, chanter Silva then led committee members to the Kalākaua crypt, where the remains of Queen Lili'uokalani lie in peaceful repose among her family. There, *ho'okupu,* prayers, chants, songs and many tears flowed together in an unabashed expression of sorrow and love for Hawai'i's last monarch.

Emerging from the crypt, committee members felt blessed and ready to open the observance activities.

'ONIPA'A
FIVE DAYS
IN THE
HISTORY
OF THE
HAWAIIAN
NATION

1893-1993

The People's Cafe in downtown Honolulu was a perfect setting for a *Pā'ina* of the 'Onipa'a Centennial Committee before the Ka Mōhala Nui, or formal opening ceremonies. Going over last-minute details are *(clockwise from left)* Chair Eloise Ululani Tungpalan, committee member Rockne Freitas, OHA officer Scotty Bowman and committee members Wendy Roylo-Hee, Mike Crozier and Leinā'ala Heine. (Elizabeth Pa Martin photo)

Wearing a traditional Hawaiian *muʻumuʻu*, ʻOnipaʻa Committee Chair Eloise Ululani Tungpalan arrives with Momi Cazimero and ʻAhahui Kaʻahumanu Society President Margaret Kula Stafford at Mauna ʻAla for services in the Royal Mausoleum. (Elizabeth Pa Martin photo)

Lydia Nāmahana Maioho, curator of the Royal Mausoleum at Mauna ʻAla, greets participants as they arrive for services at this special spiritual ceremony seeking the blessings from the royal *kūpuna*. (Elizabeth Pa Martin photo)

A solemn crowd fills the Kalākaua crypt to watch as ʻOnipaʻa Committee members present their *hoʻokupu* to Queen Liliʻuokalani. (Elizabeth Pa Martin photo)

'Onipa'a Committee member Wendy Roylo-Hee carries the Committee's *ho'okupu* to Queen Lili'uokalani at the Royal Mausoleum. She is accompanied by Royal Order of Kamehameha's Ali'i 'Aimoku, Edward Ka'ōpūiki. (Elizabeth Pa Martin photo)

'ONIPA'A
FIVE DAYS
IN THE
HISTORY
OF THE
HAWAIIAN
NATION

1893-1993

Kupuna Elizabeth Ellis leads other members of the Women's Auxiliary of the Royal Order of Kamehameha from the Kalākaua crypt at Mauna 'Ala. (Elizabeth Pa Martin photo)

OPENING CEREMONY
JANUARY 13, 1993, 12:00 NOON

The traditional blowing of the conch shell at precisely noon, January 13, 1993, signaled to the more than 2,000 people gathered in downtown Honolulu that the 'Onipa'a centennial observance had officially opened. Assembled before the stately bronze statue of Queen Lili'uokalani located between 'Iolani Palace and the State Capitol, the audience listened as *Ha'i 'Ōlelo* Palani Vaughan, master of ceremonies, opened the program for the Committee.

The ceremonies began with Christian prayers offered by Reverends William Kaina and Darrow Aiona, mingled with ancient and sacred *oli* delivered by John Keolamaka'āinanakalāhuino-Kamehameha'ekolu Lake and Wendell Ka-lani-kapu-'ae-nui Silva. These chants ceremonially honored the Queen's spiritual presence and blessed all

At the stroke of noon, Richard Bell, wearing traditional Hawaiian white shirt and trousers, red sash, and royal cape, blows the conch shell signaling the commencement of ceremonies. (Russell Ho photo)

activities that were to follow.

Sam Ka'ai then lit four large bamboo torches held by Council of Hawaiian Organizations President Melvin Kalāhiki and other officers in dignified remembrance of the fire-burning *kapu* established in ancient times by high chief Iwikauikaua. This *kapu* passed as an ancestral inheritance to Queen Lili'uokalani from her *mākua*. The four torches were posted on both sides of the Queen's statue. The fire of these flames would be ritually transferred after the ceremony to a site near the statue of Kamehameha I. There, the Council of Hawaiian Organizations would begin a 100-hour torch-burning vigil through the close of the observance.

The crowd continued to swell, completely circling the Queen's statue, filling the walking mall and spilling into the 'Iolani Palace grounds under the banyan tree. Invited dignitaries included federal, state, and city elected officials; state and city government officials and staffers; Office of Hawaiian Affairs trustees and staffers; and international guests such as prime ministers from the Cook Islands, Tonga, and Vanuatu, and foreign consuls representing Australia, France, and Switzerland. Also joining the opening ceremonies, was a diverse crowd of Hawaiian pro-sovereignty activists, musicians and singers, Hawaiian civic club and royal society members and a thousand more people from all walks of life.

In her welcoming address, 'Onipa'a Chair Eloise Ululani Tungpalan set the tone that would prevail throughout the 'Onipa'a observance. Fully acknowl-

**'Onipa'a Chair, Senator Eloise Ululani Tungpalan, presenting her welcoming address.
(Russell Ho photo)**

Wendell Ka-lani-kapu-'ae-nui Silva, 'Onipa'a Committee member and executive director of the Hawai'i State Foundation for Culture and the Arts, delivers three chants of significance — to clear the path, to honor the Queen, and to bless the people. (Russell Ho photo)

Leaders from several Pacific islands attended the opening ceremonies, including Prime Minister Baron Vaea of Tonga (*right foreground*) and Prime Minister Geoffrey Henry of the Cook Islands (*sitting to the left*). Governor John Waihe'e (*center*) greets "Aunty" Aggie Cope and the late John Dominis Holt (*holding the umbrella*). (OHA photo by Deborah Ward)

'ONIPA'A
FIVE DAYS
IN THE
HISTORY
OF THE
HAWAIIAN
NATION

1893-1993

edging the illegality of the events of a century ago and their legacy of pain, she also emphasized the importance of Hawaiians working harmoniously toward sovereignty in order to preserve their beloved heritage and race. This historic observance was to be a period of honestly facing the past while patiently seeking unity in the present.

John Waihe'e, first elected governor of Hawaiian ancestry, then stepped to the podium to announce his decision that only the Hawaiian flag would fly above all state facilities encircling 'Iolani Palace. His order solemnly and courageously honored the Hawaiian Kingdom. For the first time in nearly 100 years, only the standard of Hawai'i would grace the Capitol district. Applause from the gathered assembly enthusiastically greeted the Governor's announcement as the importance of this symbolic gesture stirred a heightened sense that history was indeed in the making.

Stirring messages from U.S. Senator Daniel Inouye and from the first elected U.S. Senator of Hawaiian ancestry, Daniel Akaka, were then read by master of ceremonies Vaughan. Akaka's message announced that for the duration of the 'Onipa'a observance, he had succeeded in arranging for the unprecedented half-staff lowering of the Hawaiian

Ha'i 'Ōlelo Palani Vaughan opens the ceremonies by explaining that the bamboo torches honor Queen Lili'uokalani. Upon the death of her brother, King Kalākaua, Lili'uokalani inherited the throne of Hawai'i. Like him, she was heir, from her ancient chiefly ancestor Iwikauikaua, to the sacred right to burn torches at mid-day. Hawaiian chanter John Keolamaka'āinanakalāhuino-Kamehameha'ekolu Lake prepares to chant an *oli* honoring Iwikauikaua, from whom he also descends. (Russell Ho photo)

(Facing page) The Hawaiian flag flies high above the capitol of Hawai'i, just as it did 100 years ago over the sovereign Hawaiian Kingdom. (*Advertiser* photo by Carl Viti)

'ONIPA'A
PREPARING TO
ENCOUNTER
HISTORY

flag in Washington, D.C. The Hawaiian flag would fly at half-staff, for the duration of the observance, at Union Station where all 50 state flags are raised together. Messages from U.S. Congressman Neil Abercrombie and Mayor Frank F. Fasi were also read. U.S. Congresswoman Patsy Mink offered glowing expressions of support for the Hawaiian people and spoke of the injustice to the deposed Queen. Office of Hawaiian Affairs Trustee Chairman Clayton Hee then spoke of the solemnity of the occasion, the importance of remembrance, and the need to end a "century of dishonor" by seeking the justice denied the Queen 100 years before.

The music of Queen Liliʻuokalani was next introduced into the ceremony as *Haʻi ʻŌlelo* Vaughan sang and translated the "Queen's Prayer." Composed by the Queen during her eight-month imprisonment in ʻIolani Palace, the beloved hymn recalls the spiritual faith that had sustained the Queen during her time of humiliation. Office of Hawaiian Affairs Trustee Kamaki Kanahele performed a moving rendition of a 100-year-old chant entitled "Makalapua," which was composed by his great-grandmother, Naha Hakuʻole, for Queen Liliʻuokalani. It had not been performed in public since his great-grandmother's presentation 100 years ago.

Larry Mehau and his family offered their musical *hoʻokupu,* with Don Ho singing "Kaulana Nā Pua," as Leo Anderson Akana interpreted this famous song of Hawaiian patriotic pride. Brickwood Galuteria and the Royal Hawaiian Band performed "Aloha ʻOe," while ʻOnipaʻa Committee members placed 100 flowers in the *ʻumeke* (calabash) at the foot of the Queen's statue. Each blossom represented one year since the overthrow of the Queen.

The ceremonies were concluded by Jeffery Apaka, son of the late, great singer Alfred Apaka, Jr., singing the moving "ʻO Makalapua" to the accompaniment of the Royal Hawaiian Band. As this musical tribute to the Queen was performed, everyone in the audience was invited to present a floral *hoʻokupu.* The people then streamed forward, hundreds of garlands being draped with love upon the statue of the Queen as "ʻO Makalapua" was played at least 10 times over and over. In the bright

26

ʻONIPAʻA
FIVE DAYS
IN THE
HISTORY
OF THE
HAWAIIAN
NATION

1893-1993

Hawaiʻi Governor John Waiheʻe announces his decision, with U.S. State Department approval, to fly only the Hawaiian flag in the Capitol district during the remaining four days of the ʻOnipaʻa Centennial Observance. (Elizabeth Pa Martin photo)

U.S. Congresswoman Patsy Mink addresses the opening ceremony audience. (Russell Ho photo)

Office of Hawaiian Affairs Chairman Clayton Hee delivers a stirring message on behalf of his fellow trustees. (Russell Ho photo)

Ho'okupu are placed at the statue of Queen Lili'uokalani by Myron Thompson, chair of Princess Bernice Pauahi Bishop Estate's Board of Trustees, his wife Laura, and Ho'alikū Drake, director of the state's Department of Hawaiian Home Lands.
(Elizabeth Pa Martin photo)

'Onipa'a patron Larry Mehau returns to his seat after laying his floral ho'okupu at the statue of Queen Lili'uokalani. (Elizabeth Pa Martin photo)

The chant "Makalapua" is performed for the first time in 100 years by Kamaki Kanahele, 'Onipa'a Committee member and Office of Hawaiian Affairs trustee. The oli kapu or sacred chant was composed by his grandmother, Naha Haku'ole, for Queen Lili'uokalani.
(Russell Ho photo)

noonday sun the bronze image of the Queen glistened amid the green *maile*, orange *'ilima* and *kukunaokalā*, yellow *'awapuhi*, white *pīkake*, and purple orchids.

As the 'Onipa'a opening ceremony came to a close, dignitaries and the general public enjoyed punch and special cakes which featured the 'Onipa'a logo. One of these cakes was sent to Lunalilo Home, a care facility for elderly Hawaiians, so that *kūpuna* unable to attend the downtown activities could participate in a small way in these significant events.

The throngs had begun to thin from the area about the Queen's statue by mid-afternoon, though some still lingered to indulge their private thoughts, or to photograph the adorned statue or to offer a prayer. The *aloha* remained in the *'umeke* cala-bash overflowing with blossoms (*nā pua*) from the opening ceremony. At sunset, the flowers were conveyed to the resting place of Queen Lili'uokalani at Mauna 'Ala by the Royal Order of Kamehameha society, its Women's Auxiliary and the Pearl Harbor Hawaiian Civic Club.

No flower that was offered during 'Onipa'a as *ho'okupu* to the Queen's statue was left unattended. Each night, every flower and *lei* were taken to the resting place of the Queen by the Royal Order of Kamehameha and its Women's Auxiliary. The love of her subjects had not waned, their devotion for Lili'uokalani having persevered over the century.

28

'ONIPA'A
FIVE DAYS
IN THE
HISTORY
OF THE
HAWAIIAN
NATION

1893-1993

The late Mrs. Mary Purdy Waihe'e, the mother of Governor Waihe'e, joined thousands of other Hawaiians during the centennial activities in proudly displaying the 'Onipa'a ribbon.
(Elizabeth Pa Martin photo)

The sight of 100 torchbearers moving through the darkened grounds of ʻIolani Palace later that evening produced an eerie sense that spirits past and present had united in the vigil of a nation. Organized by the Council of Hawaiian Organizations under President Melvin Kalāhiki, the procession had begun at Kawaiahaʻo Church at 6:45 p.m. The bamboo torches carried the Iwikauikaua flame which was marched through the grounds of ʻIolani Palace to the statue of Kamehameha I, illuminating these historic sites that 100 years before had been the setting for the overthrow of a kingdom.

The transfer of the flame was conducted in solemn ritual to the sounds of conch shells and the beating of *pahu* drums echoing 100 years of sorrow and pain for the Hawaiian people since the overthrow. With the completion of the procession, the Council of Hawaiian Organizations began a 100-hour vigil commemorating the last 100 hours of the Hawaiian monarchy. Council members joined in the vigil to perpetuate the essence of being Hawaiian through present and future generations:

The Council of Hawaiian Organizations keeps alive the steady faith and pride of our illustrious ancestors.

We follow in the wake of those brilliant Polynesian seafarers who discovered the secrets of the universe and found a holistic home through the intimate marriage of the heavens, islands and depths of the sea.

In this time of centennial reflection, the Council of Hawaiian Organizations reaffirms Hawaiʻi and walks today upon the very bones of Kulāiwi, our ancestral lands.

We call on the Hawaiian people to resolve that pono, justice shall prevail.

We call on the Hawaiian people to renew the ea, collective spirit of deep appreciation and regard for our cultural legacy.

We will be sustained for generations to come as we, like the ancient navigators, point the way for our keiki, the children of our land.

May they, too, follow the paths of their ancestors and soar freely through the limitless galaxies of future discovery, exploration and understanding.

Rarely in recent years had the cadences of the traditional drumming of the *pahu* been heard to beat so melancholy a dirge, the rhythmic throb in the torchlit night signaling the death of a nation's independence at the hands of an unjust revolution. A civilization rich in heritage, admired for its values of *aloha* and *ʻohana*, had been dispossessed of its own land. A people who measured their ancestry through the *Kumulipo*, their genesis to the origins of the earth, to the first man and woman, had been deprived of their own native rule. The long preparation for ʻOnipaʻa had concluded, the first day blessings received, as the descendants of this magnificent civilization, with other friends of the truth, prepared to seek their answers by looking into the face of history.

30

'ONIPA'A
FIVE DAYS
IN THE
HISTORY
OF THE
HAWAIIAN
NATION

1893-1993

Two of the torches lit during the opening ceremonies are taken to the site of the 100-hour vigil near Ali'iōlani Hale. A total of four torches would be placed near the Kamehameha statue, forming a straight line with the statue of Queen Lili'uokalani. (Elizabeth Pa Martin photo)

Inside the vigil tent, a *ho'okupu* table with a portrait of Queen Lili'uokalani receives the many offerings and prayers of the Hawaiian people. (Judiciary History Center photo)

Council of Hawaiian Organizations members Winona Rubin and Louis "Buzzy" Agard reverently participate in the 100-hour vigil. (Eileen Kalāhiki photo)

Lydia Luden, Melvin Kalāhiki, and the late Kalaninuipōʻaimoku Kalāhiki (*left to right*), members of the Council of Hawaiian Organizations, stand near the opening of the *haka lele* at the 100-hour vigil site. The *haka lele* was erected for the public to place their *hoʻokupu* as a sign of love, respect and tribute to Queen Liliʻuokalani. (Eileen Kalāhiki photo)

32

'ONIPA'A
FIVE DAYS
IN THE
HISTORY
OF THE
HAWAIIAN
NATION

1893-1993

Dressed in traditional attire, Sam Kaʻai leads the crowd from the ʻIolani Palace to the Kamehameha statue as David Kalama and his video crew record for the ʻOnipaʻa Centennial Committee. (Judiciary History Center photo)

A large crowd joins the torchbearers on the evening of January 13, 1993 as they gathered around the statue of Kamehameha at Aliʻiōlani Hale. (Judiciary History Center photo)

CHAPTER THREE

January 14-15, 1893: A Constitution Deferred; A Revolution Plotted

As we prepare for a series of events to remember and reflect on this dark page of our nation's history, I would hope that the people of Hawai'i, both Native Hawaiians and non-natives, would join together in a common cause for action. I have long maintained that the overthrow of the Queen was illegal. It is clear that the United States knowingly participated in the wrongful overthrow of the Hawaiian Monarchy, in violation of national and international law. As a result, Native Hawaiians have suffered immeasurably.

The native people of Hawai'i yielded to a superior force under protest but they have maintained, and I have long recognized, that the illegal action did not extinguish their sovereignty.

Daniel K. Inouye
Senator, U.S. Congress

'ONIPA'A
FIVE DAYS
IN THE
HISTORY
OF THE
HAWAIIAN
NATION

1893-1993

The Queen's Royal Guard in full dress performs military exercises in front of the barracks on the grounds of the 'Iolani Palace in 1892. Serving several Hawaiian monarchs, the Guard in their British-style uniforms had been willing, if called upon, to defend Lili'uokalani with the force of arms against the conspirators who sought to topple her government. The Queen, however, sought to avoid bloodshed in her Kingdom. (Hawai'i State Archives photo)

A CONSTITUTION DEFERRED; A REVOLUTION PLOTTED

Queen Liliʻuokalani had looked forward to Saturday, January 14, 1893 as the day which would mark the end of the despised Bayonet Constitution and the restitution of native rights and royal prerogatives under a new constitution. The morning sky sparkled blue and bright over Honolulu, perhaps portending a new era in native sovereignty as the Legislature prepared to adjourn.

Stockholders of C. Brewer & Co., who met that morning for their quarterly meeting, spread the rumor that Queen Liliʻuokalani was preparing a new constitution, but they were not inclined to believe it.

At the same time, the Queen was informing her newly selected four-man Cabinet that it was true—she intended to promulgate a new constitution later that same day.

A little before noon, cannon from the Punchbowl battery boomed a royal salute. Liliʻuokalani stepped from ʻIolani Palace, a coronet of diamonds atop her head. The long train of her gown was carried by four footmen in knee britches.

She rode in an open carriage to the legislative hall in Aliʻiōlani Hale, the government building that today is home to the Hawaiʻi Supreme Court. Attending the Queen in the royal procession across King Street were *kāhili* bearers, Oʻahu Governor Archibald Cleghorn in a uniform decorated with gold braid and military orders, the Queen's chamberlain and his staff, princesses, ladies in waiting and the ministers of government. The Royal Hawaiian Band accompanied the procession.

At Aliʻiōlani Hale, the household guards stood at attention. Ushers escorted members of the public to the upstairs gallery. The Queen took her seat, the chair topped with a regal feather cloak as if it were a throne. About 40 members of the Hui Kālaiʻāina, the Native Hawaiian political society in support of the monarchy, were resplendent in black broadcloth suits and tall silk hats. Also present were American Consul General H.W. Severance and U.S. Navy Lt. Lucien Young, in full dress uniform.

The Queen saw immediately that white lawmakers were absent, which she took as an omen of "some coming trouble." *Ka Leo O Ka Lāhui*, the Hawaiian-language newspaper, said Hawaiian leaders were "embarrassed and pained" by the absence of the whites who had absented themselves in protest of the Queen's new Cabinet. The Hawaiians said they would "be very happy to not see their sort" in the next Legislature, which would convene in 1894.

At noon, the Queen stood at the rostrum to speak, first in English, then in Hawaiian. She complimented lawmakers for passing numerous bills and liberal appropriations, and spoke of her having promoted treaty relations with "our great and friendly neighbor, the United States of America."

Adapted from "Day by Day Account of the 1893 Overthrow," *Honolulu Advertiser*, by Stu Glauberman.

36

ʻONIPAʻA
FIVE DAYS
IN THE
HISTORY
OF THE
HAWAIIAN
NATION

1893-1993

Queen Lili'uokalani leaves Ali'iōlani Hale on January 14, 1893 after proroguing the Legislature.
(Hedemann Collection, Bishop Museum photo)

The 13-member Committee of Public Safety is formed on January 14, 1893 to prevent the Queen from promulgating a new constitution which will restore the prerogatives of the monarch and extend voting rights to Hawaiians. Pictured in this commemorative display are Henry E. Cooper (chairman), Henry Waterhouse, Lorrin A. Thurston, Ed Suhr (who replaced H. F. Glade), F. W. McChesney, John Emmeluth (who replaced Albert S. Wilcox), William R. Castle, William O. Smith, John A. McCandless, Crister Bolte, William C. Wilder, Andrew Brown and Theodore F. Lansing.
(Hawai'i State Archives photo).

'ONIPA'A
FIVE DAYS
IN THE
HISTORY
OF THE
HAWAIIAN
NATION

1893-1993

Captain Samuel Nowlein was the royalist commander of the Royal Guard during the turbulent days of January 1893. (Hawai'i State Archives photo)

At a reception that followed in an adjoining chamber, guests were informed by chamberlain James Robertson that an important meeting would take place that afternoon. The Queen returned to 'Iolani Palace, accompanied by Native Hawaiian lawmakers and supporters marching two-by-two with banners.

While she waited in the Blue Room for her Cabinet, word spread through the streets that a revolution was in progress. A large crowd gathered at the Palace, where about 60 troops of the Household Guard had formed a line from the steps to the Richards Street gate. The guard stood ready, belts full of bullets. Inside, lawmakers, princes, ladies of the court and Supreme Court justices waited.

Meanwhile, U.S. Minister in Hawai'i John L. Stevens and the British government commissioner, Maj. James H. Wodehouse, met with the Queen's Cabinet. Wodehouse advised the Queen's ministers to prevent her from promulgating a new constitution that would accede to Native Hawaiian de-

mands. Stevens denounced the Legislature for having passed an Opium Bill he called "a direct attack on the United States." The bill, supported by Native Hawaiian lawmakers and opposed by *haole* lawmakers, authorized granting of a government license for $30,000 that would enable the licensee to import and sell the drug at smoking dens, but not to Hawaiians or Japanese.

As soon as the diplomats left the government building, the Cabinet members joined the Queen in the Blue Room. "After our arrival," said Finance Minister William Cornwell, "the Queen stated to us that, at the request of some 8,000 of her native subjects, she had decided to promulgate a new constitution in which the grievances of her petitioning subjects would be remedied, and she asked us to sign the document with her." In a word, the Queen's Native Hawaiian subjects wanted the powers of the monarchy restored, which meant a lessening of the influence of the business class.

"Each one of us got up, one after the other," Interior Minister John Colburn later recalled, "and told her we could not accede to her wishes, and advised her to abandon the idea." Lili'uokalani was disappointed to learn they would not back her, despite their earlier pledges of support. "I was surprised when the Cabinet informed me that they did not think it advisable for me to take such a step, that there was a danger of an uprising," she said. After advising the Queen to think it over, Colburn and Cornwell went off to discuss the situation further with diplomats and business leaders representing the foreign element.

At 3:00 p.m., the ministers returned, unyielding in their opposition, even though they said they sensed a tide of popular sentiment favoring the Queen. Cornwell said, "We earnestly advised her to give up her intention, although we were well aware that more than two-thirds of the electors of the country were in favor of the change, and that nearly all the representatives in the Legislature were elected on a platform in which the main plank was a new constitution."

After reading the proposed constitution, which resembled the earlier one Kalākaua had enjoyed,

Attorney General Arthur Peterson said the matter should be put off. Lili'uokalani felt betrayed by her advisers. "They had led me out to the edge of a precipice, and now were leaving me to take the leap alone," the Queen said. "It was humiliating."

The Queen proceeded to the Throne Room, where her guests had been waiting for three hours. "She was under great emotion," Chief Justice Albert Judd described the scene. "I never saw her in such a state of agitation. At the same time, she controlled herself."

She stepped up to the dais and informed her people of her deep regret that she could not grant them the new constitution. "Return to your homes peaceably and quietly and continue to look towards me and I will look towards you," she implored. The Hawaiian-language newspaper *Ka Leo O Ka Lāhui* explained that the Queen "wanted to fulfill the desires of her Native people, but because of the obstacles which were encountered, and because of the power of the constitution, which stood in defiance to her, she was unable to do so.

"Because of this there is *aloha* for our Queen, who tried to accomplish it under her kind thoughts...In her considered opinion it was not possible and she expressed her regret and sorrow, instructing her spokesmen on the Committee of Native People to return and wait until their desires regarding what is right could be accomplished, and asking them to preserve peace in the realm," the paper reported.

As Hui Kālai'āina chairman W.L. Holokahiki explained to the crowd outside, the Queen was "quite ready to give a new constitution, but her Cabinet (was) opposed to it. Her Cabinet refused it, so that she could not do otherwise."

Later, the Queen went out onto the second-floor balcony. Speaking in Hawaiian, she told the people to "go in good hope" and wait for her to act on the new constitution at another time. Fateful words. Her statement was translated by annexationists to mean she would try to give a new constitution in "a few days." Others, however, say her words in Hawaiian meant she was speaking of an indefinite time in the future, suggesting there was

American Minister John L. Stevens, an open supporter of American annexation of Hawai'i, was no friend of the Hawaiian monarchy which he once described as "semi-barbaric." "It must be said," wrote Queen Lili'uokalani of Minister Stevens, "that he was either mentally incapable of recognizing what is to be expected of a gentleman, to say nothing of a diplomatist, or he was decidedly in league with those persons who had conspired against the peace of Hawai'i . . ." (Bishop Museum photo)

less immediacy to the matter.

The crowd gave three cheers and began to depart behind a Hawaiian flag when Representative William White, a Hawaiian lawmaker from Lahaina, came forward to speak. According to the pro-annexationists, White made a fiery oration, calling for the deaths of the traitorous ministers who had betrayed the Queen and the Hawaiian people. But Cornwell said White merely repeated what the Queen had said, and told her followers to wait for the next Legislature.

Ex-Cabinet minister Peter Jones heard of the events later in the day. "The whole thing was like a thunderclap to the community," Jones said. Upon learning of the extraordinary goings-on at the

Palace, Honolulu merchants and tradesmen crowded into the Fort Street law offices of Judge W.O. Smith.

Supreme Court Justice Sanford B. Dole had gone sailing that morning and was walking from the wharf when he came upon the gathering, which overflowed from the three-room suite onto the street. "Both Hawaiians and white men were represented at this meeting," Dole said. "The feeling was earnest and tense, showing no disposition to brook any effort by the Queen to tamper with the constitution, or in any wise to impair its recognition of equal rights and the sovereignty of the people."

Sugar planter Charles M. Cooke wanted to know what was intended by the group's decision to form a Committee of Public Safety. "Does it mean no more Queen?" he asked. When told that's what it meant, Cooke added his name.

"The next day, which was Sunday, passed off quietly on the surface, but we had intimations that a revolutionary movement was in progress," said William deWitt Alexander, the Honolulu-born surveyor-general and professor of languages. Further evidence that something was afoot came that afternoon when posters were put up around town calling for a mass meeting of citizens on Monday at 2:00 p.m.

The call came from the Committee of Public Safety, which had met that morning. The original Committee of Safety consisted of Henry E. Cooper (chairman), Henry Waterhouse, Lorrin A. Thurston, H. F. Glade, F. W. McChesney, Albert S. Wilcox, William R. Castle, William O. Smith, John A. McCandless, Crister Bolte, William C. Wilder, Andrew Brown and Theodore F. Lansing. Within a day or two, Wilcox and Glade would resign — Wilcox to return to Kaua'i, and Glade because he was German consul. They would be replaced by Ed Suhr and John Emmeluth. Among the 13

committee members, there were four Americans, a Scot and a German, four men born in Hawai'i of American parents and three naturalized Hawaiian citizens who had come from the United States, Germany and Tasmania.

German-born Crister Bolte, a merchant and sugar company investor, said the men had resolved to prevent the Queen from having her way. "This committee met several times at various places and decided that the only perfect safeguard against future occurrences of this kind would lie in annexation to the United States, or in a protectorate or anything of that kind. But we decided not to go on with the form of government as it was then."

According to lawyer-politician W.O. Smith, the group had passed Lorrin Thurston's motion that preliminary steps be taken at once to declare a provisional government with a view toward annexation by the United States. And according to Judge Sanford Dole, "We knew that the United States minister was in sympathy with us."

At a meeting with Cabinet members at the police station, Marshall Charles Wilson proposed the arrest of the Committee of 13 for treason. Wilson was aware of their plans, having assigned special agents to tail them and watch premises that sold firearms. But Wilson was dissuaded from making arrests by Attorney General Arthur Peterson and former minister Paul Neumann, who counseled that a conflict must be avoided.

In the afternoon, the Queen's ministers learned the annexationists planned a meeting the next day at the Armory. At dinner that night, the ministers scheduled a mass meeting of their own Committee in Support of Law and Order to be held at Palace Square at the same hour, 2:00 p.m. As the Queen and her advisers worked through the night hoping to defuse the political crisis that threatened her governance, across town the cadre of businessmen prepared to seize a nation.

'ONIPA'A
FIVE DAYS
IN THE
HISTORY
OF THE
HAWAIIAN
NATION

1893-1993

CHAPTER FOUR
January 14-15, 1993
Offerings in Remembrance of Hawai'i's Queen

On January 17, 1893 Queen Lili'uokalani surrendered the throne saying she "yielded to the superior force of the United States of America . . . to avoid . . . loss of life . . . under protest . . . until such time as the Government of the United States shall . . . undo the action . . . " . . . and after yielding her throne wrote to President Harrison: "I submitted to force believing . . . you . . . will right whatever wrongs may have been inflicted upon us . . . "

That day was 100 years ago and the government of the United States is only now beginning to take notice of its responsibilities to account for this act perpetrated against the will of a sovereign people.

The United States government holds the key now as it did then.

I call upon all the people of Hawai'i to join with the Native Hawaiian people to find remedies that enjoin the past with the present, and to right these wrongs. The goal of sovereignty must be fulfilled.

Patsy T. Mink
Representative, U.S. Congress

'ONIPA'A
FIVE DAYS
IN THE
HISTORY
OF THE
HAWAIIAN
NATION

1893-1993

(Preceding page) The Royal Guard carries the Hawaiian flag past 'Iolani Palace and the Royal Hawaiian Band as they return to 'Iolani Barracks during the spiritual *ho'okupu* ceremonies. (OHA photo by Deborah Ward)

Early on the morning of January 14, 1993, for the first time in 100 years, the royal standard of Queen Lili'uokalani was raised over the nearly empty grounds of 'Iolani Palace. On this same day 100 years earlier, 'Iolani Palace had been the setting for the events which would lead to the overthrow of the monarchy. In the Blue Room, Queen Lili'uokalani informed her cabinet of her intention to promulgate a new constitution. Her ministers turned away from her and so gave impetus to the opposition. Later that day the Queen crossed the great hall to the Throne Room to make the painful announcement that she had been forced to abandon her effort at political change. She would return to the Throne Room a few days later to yield to the forces of the United States.

For the Friends of 'Iolani Palace, these moments were too powerful to be re-created in the Palace rooms. Instead, after 26 years of hunting for original furniture and reweaving fabrics, the rooms were made to be exactly as they were when Queen Lili'uokalani saw them on those days in 1893. After two more years of research, the designs for the Royal Standard and the mourning drapery for the Palace and its lamp posts and gates were rediscovered and perfectly copied. The costs of the drapery and the Royal Standard were borne entirely by the Friends of 'Iolani Palace as a gift to the people.

Representatives of Hawaiian organizations were invited to enter the Palace for a spiritual *ho'okupu*, a quiet pilgrimage into the world of their Queen, to see, to feel, to pay homage as they wished, and to remember.

At 8:00 a.m. muffled drumming was heard as the Royal Guard began a slow march from 'Iolani Barracks to their stations in front of 'Iolani Palace. The soldiers marched in an unusual way, with rifles upside-down in the manner of mourning which had been used in the last century to honor the *ali'i*. As they reached the Palace, the Guardsmen ascended the stairs to stand in honor guard formation. An *oli* was performed to honor Hawai'i's last Queen and, after brief opening words, the Palace doors were opened. The Royal Guard commander, the *Kapena Moku*, stepped forward to escort the people up the steps to the entrance. During the long, silent day, several hundred Hawaiians from all walks of life and all islands, representing a wide range of Hawaiian organizations, offered their *ho'okupu* of tears, spontaneous *oli*, and *aloha* to the Queen.

At dusk, Kaipo Farias of Hālau o Kekuhi delivered a *kanikau*, composed to express the terrible collective sorrow of *ka po'e Hawai'i* over 100 years and this was answered by a light, misty rain. The long pilgrimage of this day was concluded with an *oli* of hope delivered by Manu Boyd, and the singing of "Hawai'i Pono'i."

Gov. John Waihe'e, wearing the cloak of the Royal Order of Kamehameha, walks with Edward Kawananakoa as they carry *ho'okupu* to the statue of Queen Lili'uokalani. (*Advertiser* photo by T. Umeda)

Kaipo Farias from the island of Hawai'i offers a moving *kanikau*, chanting a lament at the closing of the spiritual *ho'okupu* event. (Elizabeth Pa Martin photo)

Ladies from Hale O Na Ali'i offer their *lei aloha* at the Queen's statue. (OHA photo by Deborah Ward)

*W*elcome to this house of sorrow,
Welcome to this time of tears.
Welcome to the silent heart of your ancient nation.
Welcome to the home of noble dreams and great hopes.

Bring your selves, and your own bitter tears.
Bring your tribute of memories and mourning.
Ka Haleali'i 'o 'Iolani awaits your footsteps, as it has for 100 years.
Come and remember what you are.

'Iolani Palace is the ceremonial home of the Ruler of the
Hawaiian people and the focus of its dreams of nationhood.
This house contained the holy treasures of the people:
the feather cloaks of sovereignty, the sacred conch trumpet, the great *Kāhili*,
the *Niho Palaoa*, the *Pūlo'ulo'u*, the Thrones and Crowns.

This house enthroned the living treasures of sacred blood,
In this house they reigned in splendor and in this house the rule of these Lords
and the independence of Hawai'i was destroyed.

One hundred years ago today, in this place, Lili'uokalani, beloved Queen, tried
to save her people and she was defeated.
Her people were thrust aside.
Her way of life, which had its origins more than sixty generations in the past,
was overturned.

It was an ending.
It was a death.
It was the casting down of a people.
It was the casting down of a Queen.
It was the destruction of a nation.
It was an ending, or so it seemed.

But against all odds, the nation persevered.
The nation lives, and it is you.

> Opening words, spiritual *ho'okupu*
> Friends of 'Iolani Palace

'ONIPA'A
FIVE DAYS
IN THE
HISTORY
OF THE
HAWAIIAN
NATION

1893-1993

As the spiritual *ho'okupu* were being offered at 'Iolani Palace, across the street at Ali'iōlani Hale, a formal ceremony by the Judiciary History Center was underway commemorating the closing of the Kingdom of Hawai'i's last legislative session. Built by Kamehameha V, Ali'iōlani Hale housed the Legislative Assembly of the Kingdom of Hawai'i until the illegal overthrow of Queen Lili'uokalani. Today, the building is the home of the state's Judiciary and its Judiciary History Center.

At noon on January 14, 1893, Queen Lili'uokalani had officially dismissed the Legislature in Ali'iōlani Hale, center of the Kingdom's govern-

Ali'iōlani Hale to witness this event with harmony of spirit and a sense of pride.

On a black velvet stand stood a regal portrait of Queen Lili'uokalani under a thick green *lei* of fresh large-leaf *maile*, white crown flowers, and yellow-orange *hala.* Close beside this place of honor, a single musician, Kikila Hugo, played gently on his guitar.

Across the rotunda sat a mixed gathering of 'Onipa'a Committee members, Office of Hawaiian Affairs trustees, Hawaiian civic club members and officers, members of the Royal Order of Kame-hameha and its Women's Auxiliary, the 'Ahahui Ka'ahumanu and others.

The Royal Guard march into the rotunda of Ali'iōlani Hale with the flag of Hawai'i as guests stand solemnly at attention. (OHA photo by Jeff Clark)

(*left to right*) Governor John Waihe'e, Lt. Governor Ben Cayetano, OHA Chair Clayton Hee, Senator Eloise Ululani Tungpalan, former Chief Justice William Richardson and Chief Justice Herman Lum participate in ceremonies commemorating the 100th anniversary of the closing of the last Legislature of the Kingdom of Hawai'i. (OHA photo by Jeff Clark)

ment for nearly 20 years. She later left Ali'iōlani Hale in her carriage and arrived at the Palace to meet with her ministers in both the Blue Room and Throne Room to discuss the promulgation of a new Hawaiian constitution which the Native Hawaiian organization Hui Kālai'āina desired her to establish.

One hundred years later, the somber and dignified tones of chanter Nathan Nāpōkā filled the halls of Ali'iōlani Hale to mark the centennial observance of the prorogation of the 1892 Legislative Assembly. Hundreds of guests representing government, Hawaiian organizations and the general public gathered at

As the opening chant concluded, the Royal Guard carried the flag of the Kingdom of Hawai'i and the Royal Standard of the Queen into the rotunda with slow, measured steps. The sonorous voice of the chanter filled the rotunda with a special *oli*, composed on March 1, 1893, by a Hawaiian woman named Noho-pono-i-ka-piko-o-nā-pua. It was a prayerful plea to the Queen to guard the Kingdom:

Among the invited guests at the Aliʻiōlani Hale ceremony are Office of Hawaiian Affairs trustees (*second row*) Rowena Akana, Abraham Aiona and Kīnaʻu Boyd Kamaliʻi. Melody McKenzie, Hawaiian Claims executive director, is sitting directly behind Trustee Aiona. (OHA photo by Jeff Clark)

ʻONIPAʻA
FIVE DAYS
IN THE
HISTORY
OF THE
HAWAIIAN
NATION

1893-1993

Hālau Nā Mamo O Puʻuanahulu, under the direction of *Kumu Hula* William Haunuʻu Ching, performs dances honoring Queen Liliʻuokalani. (OHA photo by Jeff Clark)

Nohoponoikapikoonāpua Oli

He pule, he uwalo nou e Kalani

Kāheaʻia aʻe ou kūpuna

ʻO Pele, ʻo Hiʻiaka ko Hawaiʻi

Ke ahi a mau i Maunaloa

Kānehekili[1] ko Maui ia

Ka pū nākolokolo i ka lani

ʻO Kamohoaliʻi[2] ko Kanaloa

Ke kupua nui o ka moana kai

Kāneʻāpua[3] ko Lānaʻi

Ke aliʻi kapu ia o Hanauli

Kahuilaokalani[4] ko Molokaʻi

Ke ahikao lele i ke ahiahi

Kaʻahupāhau[5] ko Oʻahu

Ke āiwaiwa ia o Puʻuloa

Manokalanipō[6] ko Kauaʻi

He akua, he aliʻi mai ka pō mai

Kūhaimoana[7] ko Niʻihau

A ʻo Kūpiopio ko Kula ia

Nā pākū ia ou paemoku

Maluhia ko aupuni a ka Lani

ʻAʻohe kipi, ʻaʻohe ʻeu

Nāna e pākaha ko Aupuni

Lilo i mea ʻole nā ʻenemi

Lanakila loa ʻo Liliʻulani,

A prayer a plea for you o Majesty

Your ancestors call out

Pele and *Hiʻiaka* of *Hawaiʻi*

The eternal fires at *Maunaloa*

Kānehekili of *Maui*

The thunderous conch of the heavens

Kamohoaliʻi of *Hanaloa*

The demigod of the deep sea

Kāneʻāpua of *Lānaʻi*

The sacred chief of *Hanauli*

Kahuilaokalani of *Molokaʻi*

The flying firebrands of the evening

Kaʻahupāhau of *Oʻahu* here

The amazing deity of *Puʻuloa*

Manokalanipō of *Kauaʻi*

A god, a chief of divine origins

Kūhaimoana of *Niʻihau*

And *Kūpiopio* of Kula

The defenders of your islands

May you have a peaceful

Kingdom, oh Chiefess

With no uprisings or rebellions

By them your Kingdom will be plundered

Let the enemies have nothing

Liliʻulani be victorious,

Hakuʻia e: Miss *Nohoponoikapikoonāpua*
Maluikeao, March 1, 1893
Translation by: Nathan Nāpōkā

FOOTNOTES

[1] God of Thunder. Literally translated; thunder *Kāne*

[2] *Peleʻs* younger brother and King of the sharks. Literally translated; the royal selected one.

[3] A fish god of *Kaunolū* village *Lānaʻi* and the name of a nearby islet. Also the name of *Peleʻs* younger brother who was deserted by *Kamohoaliʻi* on *Nihoa*. Literally translated; *Kāne* fish trap.

[4] *Peleʻs* younger brother known to dwell in the aʻe tree at *Maunaloa, Molokaʻi* where a sorcery god was carved out of this tree's wood. Literally translated; the lighting of the heavens.

[5] The chiefess of the sharks of *Puʻuloa* or Pearl Harbor. Literally translated; the well cared for garment.

[6] *Kauaʻiʻs* golden age was during the reign of chief *Manokalanipō*.

[7] A shark god brother of *Pele* who lived at *Kaʻula* islet. He was married to *Kaʻahupahau* of *Puʻuloa*. Literally translated; *Kū* following ocean.

50

'ONIPA'A
FIVE DAYS
IN THE
HISTORY
OF THE
HAWAIIAN
NATION

1893-1993

A Kamehameha Schools student smiles radiantly after her choir's performance at Ali'iōlani Hale. (Elizabeth Pa Martin photo)

Meleanna Meyer reads the list of legislators present when the Queen closed the Legislature in 1893. (Lani Ma'a Lapilio photo)

The program that followed included a dramatic reading by actress Leo Anderson Akana, a historical account of the last legislature by Association of Hawaiian Civic Clubs President H. Bruss Keppeler and the reading of the names of the representatives of the last legislative session by Meleanna Aluli Meyer. Hālau Nā Mamo o Pu'uanahulu, directed by *Kumu Hula* William Haunu'u Ching, paid homage to the past through *hula* and chant, followed by the youthful, vibrant tones of the Kamehameha Schools Children's Choir. The program ended with an outdoor concert by the Royal Hawaiian Band under the direction of Bandmaster Aaron Mahi.

A century earlier, Queen Lili'uokalani had followed the closing ceremonies at Ali'iōlani Hale with a carriage procession to 'Iolani Palace. To have re-created that procession through the "living history" program, however, would have interfered with the day of spiritual offerings taking place at the Palace. Consequently, as the ceremonies ended at noon, the re-enactment of history was postponed until the following morning.

52

'ONIPA'A
FIVE DAYS
IN THE
HISTORY
OF THE
HAWAIIAN
NATION

1893-1993

The dawn was breaking as a small group of men and women of all ethnicities gathered at the burial mound on ʻIolani Palace grounds. They were joined by the *kūpuna* to receive a special blessing and then to chant in unison to welcome the sun. For over six months, many of the group had been rehearsing for what would be perhaps the most memorable roles in their acting careers. For some of those who had never acted before, the decision to participate in the street drama testified to their commitment to the goals of the ʻOnipaʻa observance. For everyone, the opportunity to delve into historical records, exploring the lives of their different characters, opened their eyes to new perspectives on the events of 1893.

The first re-enactment scene was performed in the morning on the Palace grounds, culminating the efforts of hundreds of actors, costumers, support staff, peacekeepers and family and friends. The audience crowded in to listen to the "citizens" of 1893 Hawaiʻi share their thoughts and sentiments concerning the momentous political events about to unfold. The crowds continued to grow during the day as the free performances, staged whenever possible in the actual places where history took place a century earlier, educated and enthralled them. No classroom history lesson could have been more effective than a meeting with the people of the past — some famous, others anonymous. Through the re-enactment drama, current generations could be linked to the men and women who had lived through those extraordinary days.

(Facing page) The royal standard of the Kalākaua dynasty flies over ʻIolani Palace for the first time in 100 years. (*Advertiser* photo by Carl Viti)

Dallas Mossman Vogeler leads the members of Hui Naʻauao's Board of Directors, the "Overthrow" street theater actors and spectators in a moment of prayer as dawn rises over Honolulu. Following the dedication ceremony, each actor received a special *pōhaku* wrapped with Hawaiian salt in *ti* leaf as *hoʻokupu* to keep while portraying the historical figures of 1893. Sitting in the *koa* chair draped with a Hawaiian quilt is *kupuna* Elizabeth Nālani Ellis, who opened the drama by portraying a Hawaiian elder telling the story of the overthrow of Queen Liliʻuokalani. (Elizabeth Pa Martin photo)

The generation-to-generation contact was manifest in many ways. Before noon a large group of Roosevelt High School students marched to ʻIolani Palace to present their elegantly crafted *lei hulu*. This project was sponsored by the ʻOnipaʻa Centennial Committee whose goals included the involvement of the youth of Hawaiʻi in the process of understanding the overthrow of 1893 and its effect on the lives of contemporary Hawaiians. When the march was announced earlier that year, teachers at Roosevelt High School had been touched by the overwhelming student response to calls for *kōkua*. A few students who were close to dropping out of school were so committed to the project that they came to school every day. The spirit of these Roosevelt High School students was inspiring to all who observed their dignified march.

The value of this kind of participation was evident to teachers throughout Oʻahu. Students from several other high schools also marched to the 'Iolani Palace to join in centennial activities. Among them were students from Peter Lonoae'a's Hawaiian Studies class at Campbell High School, who participated in sign-holding as part of their study of the centennial of the overthrow of the Hawaiian monarchy.

The power of "living history" as an educational tool for young and old was evident at noon, when the Queen's historic January 14, 1893 procession from Ali'iōlani Hale to 'Iolani Palace was re-enacted. Thousands of onlookers crowded onto the grounds as King Street was blocked to allow the Queen's carriage access to the gates. With Royal Guard escort, historically costumed ministers, supporters, and subjects, the scene was an uncanny re-creation of the past as hats and caps were instinctively doffed out of respect to the Queen. This first appearance of the Queen, performed by Leo

Anderson Akana, represented pageantry on a new scale; members of the crowd stretched their necks and stood on tip-toe to see it. From the Palace steps, the Queen explained that her new constitution had met with obstacles and could not be presented. She implored her people to return to their homes peacefully, so she could prepare to grant them a constitution at some later time. At that point, the drama felt like the reality of a century ago. Later that day, the tension mounted as the crowd was introduced to the Committee of Public Safety which had been formed to oppose the Queen and the sovereign government of Hawai'i. Rumors were afoot that on the following day, the "citizens of the Kingdom" would return to the Palace grounds to witness the Committee of 13 work with U.S. Minister Stevens to force the Hawaiian government into open political confrontation.

54

'ONIPA'A
FIVE DAYS
IN THE
HISTORY
OF THE
HAWAIIAN
NATION

1893-1993

The Committee of Public Safety meets with U.S. Minister John L. Stevens to receive his guarantee of support during a re-enactment of history. Minister Stevens (*left*, played by Bill Ogilvie), joins A.S. Hartwell (played by Tom Hopcroft), W.O. Smith (played by Stephen Hancock), Lorrin A. Thurston (played by Samuel Zap) and Henry Waterhouse (played by David Eyre) to plot of the overthrow of the Hawaiian monarch. (*Advertiser* photo by Bruce Asato)

As the audience presses in to re-live history, drama director Dallas Mossman Vogeler introduces the first scene in which the Queen's loyal subjects portrayed by (*left to right*) Leonard Stolfi, Karen Loebl, Kiʻilei Balaz and Matthew Gorton (*rear*) discuss the political crisis in the kingdom. (Elizabeth Pa Martin photo)

Nālani Olds reminds the crowd that the Queen asks that a peaceful attitude be maintained by all. (Elizabeth Pa Martin photo)

OFFERINGS IN
REMEMBRANCE
OF HAWAIʻI'S
QUEEN

Glen Grant plays a historic "narrator" who rallies the people to support the Queen as she prepares to announce their new constitution. (Elizabeth Pa Martin photo)

56

'ONIPA'A
FIVE DAYS
IN THE
HISTORY
OF THE
HAWAIIAN
NATION

1893-1993

Leo Akana as the Queen is helped into her carriage by Edward Ka'ōpūiki, Ali'i 'Aimoku of the Royal Order of Kamehameha Chapter I. (Lani Ma'a Lapilio photo)

Roosevelt High School students are greeted by Governor John Waihe'e as they present their *ho'okupu* at 'Iolani Palace. (Elizabeth Pa Martin photo)

Chanting Ka Lāhui members marching into 'Iolani Palace. (OHA photo by Deborah Ward)

58

'ONIPA'A
FIVE DAYS
IN THE
HISTORY
OF THE
HAWAIIAN
NATION

1893-1993

Tāne Fernandez, a Campbell High School student, stands along King Street encouraging passersby to remember the overthrow of Queen Lili'uokalani and support the return of Kaho'olawe to the Hawaiian people. (*Advertiser* photo by Carl Viti)

CHAPTER FIVE

January 16, 1893: The Invasion of a Kingdom

Of all the wrongs committed against the Hawaiian people as a result of the overthrow, none was more painful than the loss of Hawaiian lands. A bitter fate for a nation whose motto is Ua Mau Ke Ea O Ka ʻĀina I Ka Pono—The life of the Land is Perpetuated in Righteousness.

Now it is time to correct that injustice. The solution is obvious: Return Hawaiian lands to Hawaiian hands.

As Hawaiian lands are returned to the Hawaiian people, their rightful owners, so will justice be served. Hawaiian lands in Hawaiian hands: let these words be our touchstone. They will be the measure of our success.

Neil Abercrombie
Representative, U.S. Congress

60

'ONIPA'A
FIVE DAYS
IN THE
HISTORY
OF THE
HAWAIIAN
NATION

1893-1993

The Infantry Company
of the *U.S.S. Boston* was
stationed at the U.S.
Legation and the U.S.
Consul. (Hawai'i State
Archives photo)

Troops of the *U.S.S. Boston* stand at attention with Gatling guns at Camp Boston, Honolulu, Hawai'i. The invasion of Hawai'i began on the evening of Monday, January 16, 1893. (Bishop Museum photo)

On the evening of January 16, U.S. military troops were bivouacked at Arion Hall which was located on Mililani Street near 'Iolani Palace. This photograph of Mililani Street, looking toward the King Street entrance of the Palace grounds, shows Arion Hall to the left and Ali'iōlani Hale to the right. The building between Arion Hall and King Street is the Opera House. The positioning of this large detachment of troops so close to the government buildings of the capital of the Hawaiian Kingdom raised concern over their supposed intentions to "protect American property" which was situated on the other side of town. (Hawai'i State Archives photo)

January 16, 1893

O n the morning of Monday, January 16, 1893, businesses, shops, schools and marketplaces opened up as if it were any first day of the week. Despite all of the political rallies and intrigues of the weekend, men, women and children went about their business as usual. Few of the citizens of the town realized that, behind the scenes, maneuvers were taking place which would overturn the government of the kingdom.

By noon that day, the ministers circulated a placard expressing their appreciation for "the quiet and order which has prevailed in this community since the events of Saturday" and apologizing on behalf of the Queen, who they said "was under the stress of her native subjects."

"Authority is given for the assurance that any changes desired in the fundamental law of the land will be sought only by methods provided in the constitution itself."

The Hawaiian-language newspaper *Ka Leo O Ka Lāhui* reported on Monday morning that the meeting at the Armory was being convened by "missionaries of the Reform Circle, and the people who deceive them, with the intention of criticizing the Queen for her loving care of the native people and for her agreeing to announce the new constitution, in order to take her from the throne and turn this kingdom into a republic." The newspaper advised Native Hawaiians not to attend, even if invited. "All of you true Hawaiians, we must support our Sovereign, and sacrifice our lives for the good of our Queen and for the peace of this land." It urged Hawaiians to support their chiefs by standing in Palace Square "until weary." "We must unite as one heart of *aloha* all the breasts from each corner of the land, O, descendants of Kamehameha!"

Marshal Wilson said about 3,000 people attended the rally in support of the Queen in the little square across from the Palace, although the annexationists said only a thousand attended. If fireworks were expected, none were launched by the Queen's most vocal supporters. Among them were the Hawaiian leaders Joseph Nāwahī, Robert W. Wilcox and William White. "It was a tame and dispirited meeting," observed Professor Alexander. "It seemed unnatural to hear R. W. Wilcox and Bill White exhort the natives to keep quiet and not to provoke the *haoles* to resort to violent measures."

Ka Leo O Ka Lāhui reported that the commoners adopted a resolution with delight, to the effect that they supported the Queen and accepted her word that she will not try to change the constitution by revolutionary means. "Because of this unity, the actions to overthrow the kingdom by people greedy for power, shall perhaps fail," the newspaper concluded. Wilcox delivered the resolution to the Queen. Minister Samuel Parker served the assembly champagne.

Adapted from "Day by Day Account of the 1893 Overthrow," *Honolulu Advertiser* by Stu Glauberman.

'ONIPA'A
FIVE DAYS
IN THE
HISTORY
OF THE
HAWAIIAN
NATION

1893-1993

An Infantry Company of the *U.S.S. Boston* drills at Palace Square on King Street. Their presence in Honolulu was later condemned by President Grover Cleveland as "wholly without justification." (Hawai'i State Archives photo)

Even as troops were landing in response to what U.S. Minister Stevens called "critical circumstances" in Honolulu, the Royal Hawaiian Band under conductor Henri Berger was performing a concert at the nearby Hawaiian Hotel. For a community described by the U.S. Minister as being on the threshold of violence with "inadequate legal force," conditions did not curtail a lovely evening concert by the kingdom's beloved band, pictured here on the steps of 'Iolani Palace. (Hawai'i State Archives photo)

The Queen's public apology and assurances were not sufficient to deter the annexationists, who had found in the aborted constitution an event to rally against. As the day progressed, business activity on the streets of Honolulu slowed and eventually ceased. The main business houses closed to allow owners and clerks to attend the mass meeting called by the Committee of Safety at the Honolulu Rifles Armory, known to many as the Skating Rink. The Armory was located on Beretania Street near Punchbowl Street, roughly where the state's Kalanimoku office building now stands.

"As 2 o'clock drew near, all business was suspended, stores were closed and but one subject was talked of," wrote Professor Alexander. He estimated the crowd at more than 1,500, although Marshal Wilson's police said there were between 500 and 600 people present. The American physician Francis Day described the crowd as "white men of the community, mostly of all classes and nationalities."

'ONIPA'A
FIVE DAYS
IN THE
HISTORY
OF THE
HAWAIIAN
NATION

1893-1993

Steamship company owner William C. Wilder, who headed the committee, called the meeting to order, saying, "We meet here today as men, not of any party, faction or creed, but as men who are bound to see good government." Wilder introduced Lorrin Thurston, who recounted the Queen's actions of two days earlier, and read a resolution calling for "the citizens of Honolulu of all nationalities and regardless of political party affiliations...to condemn and denounce the Queen and her supporters."

Ridiculing the Queen's repentance, Thurston said: "she wants us to sleep on a slumbering volcano which will some morning spew out blood and destroy us all." Thurston then challenged the men to rise to the protection of their liberties. "Has the tropic sun cooled and thinned our blood, or have we flowing in our veins the warm, rich blood which makes men love liberty and die for it?"

Others sought to emphasize the theme that the Queen was a threat to the business community. "My fellow citizens," intoned Alexander Young of the Honolulu Iron Works, "while the Queen and her Cabinet play fast and loose with the affairs of state, there can be no feeling of security for foreign families residing within these domains. There can be no business prosperity here at home and our credit abroad must be of the flimsiest and most uncertain nature."

Maui sugar planter H.P. Baldwin suggested the committee should deal with the Queen within the guidelines of the constitution. "The Queen's proclamation has not inspired confidence, but shall we not teach her to act within the constitution?" he asked. Baldwin was all but shouted down.

"The meeting adjourned about 4 o'clock in the afternoon," Dr. Day said, "(with) everyone feeling we were on the eve of a crisis." "After the mass meeting, the tension of feeling was extreme," added Professor William Alexander.

Rumors spread that angry Hawaiians intended to set fire to houses in the town that night. Members of the Committee of Public Safety circulated through the town interviewing men who were willing to take arms against the Queen.

"That evening," said Dr. Francis Day, "the news came to me that the monarchy was to be abrogated and that there was to be the establishment of a provisional form of government. I think the word was passed around pretty generally among the supporters of the Reform Party, as it was called."

The United States had kept a warship, the *U.S.S. Boston,* at Honolulu for many years with special orders to preserve the peace in the islands in the event of civil disturbance. This American warship had just returned from a cruise to Hilo and Lahaina and was moored at Naval Row a half mile out in Honolulu Harbor. Lt. Lucien Young was supervising the men when the walrus-mustachioed ship's captain, Commodore Gilbert Wiltse, sent for him. Wiltse informed the lieutenant that trouble was brewing; that the Hawaiian government could not protect the life and property of American residents.

After reviewing his confidential orders, Wiltse concluded he was authorized to land troops to preserve and protect U.S. treaty rights with the Sandwich Islands. "I think I will have to land the troops," he said. He instructed Young to prepare one of the ship's two Gatling guns and one of two revolving cannons.

During the evening hours of January 16, 1893, the Committee of Public Safety met and named an executive council for their Provisional Government.   Members of the executive council of the Provisional government are *(from left to right)* **James A. King, Sanford B. Dole, William O. Smith and Peter C. Jones. (Bishop Museum photo)**

At 3:00 p.m., the American minister, John Stevens, boarded the ship to relay the Committee of Public Safety's request for the landing of troops. The committee expressed fear that public safety was threatened. Within the hour, the *Boston*'s battalion got the order. Preparations took three-quarters of an hour. Wiltse advised his officers to be careful ashore "and remain as neutral as you can."

The battalion, which consisted of three companies of sailors, an artillery company, and a Marine company, totaled 154 men and 10 officers. It had been a common sight in Honolulu — the men usually landed once a week for drill and exercise at the baseball grounds. Local people would attend the drill as if it were a performance by a marching band. This time, however, the troops were ordered to equip themselves in heavy marching order. They left the *Boston* aboard eight boats, reaching C.

Brewer's landing at 5:00 p.m.

Carrying knapsacks and wearing double belts of cartridges, with 60 to 80 rounds of ammunition, the sailors and Marines marched up Queen Street and turned on Fort Street. With them they brought a Gatling gun with 14,000 rounds of ammunition, and a revolving cannon with 174 shells.

John Lot Kaulukou, who had attended a pro-monarchy rally, said no one knew what to think when they saw the U.S. troops land. "If you were here at that time, you could hear foreigners and natives asking this question: 'What does this mean? For what reason do these people come ashore?'"

"I said, 'Nobody knows. Perhaps they come to support the Queen's Government.'"

The sight of the Gatling gun was fearsome, Kaulukou said. "They had everything ready to meet their enemies."

The battalion's first order of business was to post a guard at the U.S. Consul General's office on Merchant Street. A Marine company of 30 or 40 men was detailed to protect the U.S. Legation, where Minister Stevens lived, on Nu'uanu Street. The main body of the troops turned and marched down King Street.

Queen Lili'uokalani was sitting alone in the Blue Room of the Palace when advisers rushed in with word that U.S. troops were approaching. "Why had they landed when everything was at peace?" she wondered. She instructed her advisers to tell people gathered outside to be quiet, and she proceeded to the balcony.

Marching among the troops, Lt. Young saw her. "As we passed the Palace, the Queen was standing on the balcony, when we gave her the royal salute by drooping the colors, and [playing] four ruffles on the drums," Young later recalled.

66

'ONIPA'A
FIVE DAYS
IN THE
HISTORY
OF THE
HAWAIIAN
NATION

1893-1993

The troops stopped for some time on the south corner of the Palace grounds, arousing the curiosity of the townspeople. Having failed to secure the nearby Music Hall as quarters, the landing force then marched on to the home of businessman J.B. Atherton on King Street near Alapa'i Street, where they rested under trees, drinking lemonade and eating bananas.

Rain was falling that evening when the troops marched back up King Street to quarters that Stevens had found for them at Arion Hall. A privately owned one-story wooden building on the oceanside of the Music Hall at the corner of Mililani and King Streets, the hall was directly across from Ali'iōlani Hale, and in full view of the Palace.

With many of the American residences and properties in Nu'uanu Valley or downtown Honolulu, the Queen wondered why the American troops were bivouacked in the heart of the government district. "I was told that it was for the safety of American citizens and the protection of their interests," she said. "Then why had they not gone to the residences, instead of drawing a line in front of the Palace gates, with guns pointed at us, and when I was living with my people in the Palace?"

At the Police Station, Marshal Charles Wilson proposed surrounding Ali'iōlani Hale with troops and exercising the arrest warrant he had prepared. Attorney General Arthur Peterson dissuaded him, saying that military confrontation would certainly mean violence and possible bloodshed.

Had the political upheavals of January 16, 1893 warranted the landing of U.S. troops to protect American lives and property? Earlier that day, the streets of Honolulu had appeared very much as usual, with women and children freely moving about in no imminent danger. Even after the troops had sealed themselves in Arion Hall, the strains of the Royal Hawaiian Band could be heard playing in town — evidently the hysteria of the situation was not great enough to cancel the concert for a group of visitors who had arrived in the islands!

During the evening, the Committee of Safety met and named an executive council for their Provisional Government. This Provisional Government would replace the lawful government of the sovereign nation of Hawai'i.

Sanford B. Dole, an associate justice of the Supreme Court of the Kingdom, was asked to serve as president of the council. Dole hesitated. He left the meeting and delivered the detailed plans of the movement to overthrow the nation to American Minister John L. Stevens' home.

As the Queen's advisers issued protests against the actions of the U.S. military, the troops settled in for the evening. Citizens of the kingdom considered courses of action to be taken in the morning to preserve the sovereignty of their nation.

CHAPTER SIX

January 16, 1993:
The Nation Gathers

Queen Liliʻuokalani gave up her government peacefully to avoid the killing of her subjects and in the hope that the illegal act would be reversed through intervention by the President and Congress of the United States. Her decision spared the lives of Hawaiians and other residents of Hawaiʻi as she inspired her people to depend solely on the law for the redress of this wrongful act. She always will be revered for her deep love of her people and her respect for the law.

Frank F. Fasi
Mayor, City & County of Honolulu

'ONIPA'A
FIVE DAYS
IN THE
HISTORY
OF THE
HAWAIIAN
NATION

1893-1993

(Previous page) The *keiki o ka'āina* perform a loving tribute to Queen Lili'uokalani during the Hawaiian music Skygate concert. (OHA photo by Jeff Clark)

The people began to assemble early on the morning of Saturday, January 16, 1993 in the Capitol district of Honolulu. A full day of activities had been scheduled for the centennial observance: Hawaiian quilting and native crafts demonstrations, a crafts fair and a musical concert were slated as well as the ongoing street drama performances, special daily ceremonies and expressions of concern for sovereignty by various Hawaiian groups. From a distance, the activities may have appeared festive — within the crowd, however, one always sensed that an extraordinary mood prevailed of pride and solemnity for the historic events these activities commemorated.

In the morning, the street drama began with a poignant visit between Queen Lili'uokalani and her subjects, followed by a meeting of the Committee of Public Safety staged on the Coronation Pavilion. So vivid were the re-enactments that disclaimers were necessary throughout the day. These re-minded the audience that the characters were only role-players. Their words were those of people of 1893 and not expressions of personal belief!

The construction of the *ahu*, or shrine, on the Palace grounds also com-menced that morning as Palikapu o Kamohoali'i Dedman, of Hawai'i island, oversaw the placement of the *pōhaku*, or stones, that had been brought to the site near the burial mound. Dedicated on January 17, 1993 under the guidance of the late Parley Kanaka'ole, the area around the *ahu* was intended to serve as a comfortable meeting place for Hawaiian groups from throughout the islands. Floral offerings would be made on the *ahu* throughout the weekend by Hawaiians showing their respect.

QUILT DEMONSTRATIONS
AND HAWAIIAN ENTREPRENEUR FAIR

For the people who had come to the Capitol district to witness the "street theater" performances and other Saturday activities, the central focus for disseminating information became the three large tents, provided courtesy of the E.K. Fernandez Shows, which were erected on the front lawn of the main branch of the Library of Hawai'i, with the permission of Bart Kane, the director of state libraries. On both Saturday and Sunday, this area served as the center for traditional Hawaiian arts and crafts demonstrations and displays, as well as Information Central for various groups concerned with Hawaiian issues.

Under the tents, information tables were set up and various specialists were present to answer questions about services and organizations for Hawaiians. This gathering offered an excellent opportunity to broaden the awareness of islanders of all ethnic backgrounds on the social and cultural issues that concern the Hawaiian communities.

Hawaiian quilting techniques were demonstrated by master quilter Deborah Kepola Kakalia, supported by her family and students. Her husband, David, showed his skills in basting the *lau* or pattern to the backing. Moana Espinda wove baskets, trays, containers, and other items from the coconut palm frond. Ethelreda Kahalewai, of the Royal Feather Company, displayed the various types of feather adornments once created by ancient Hawaiians and being replicated today. Julia Toomey spoke about the various types of edible seaweed or *limu* found in the waters surrounding the islands. She also showed the use of a *lomi* stick. Beatrix Crowell made traditional style fresh flower *lei*, while Rose Gahan wove *lauhala* and demonstrated *poi* pounding techniques. Duncan Ka'ohu Seto, a Honolulu fire fighter, displayed his unique skills as an expert *lauhala* weaver.

The arts and skills of the Hawaiian civilization

Master Quilter Deborah Kepola Kakalia explains the art of Hawaiian quilting. (Annelore Niejahr photo)

demonstrated a mastery in the use of available resources to fashion objects of outstanding beauty and usefulness. Thousands of people, Hawaiian and non-Hawaiian alike, watched, asked questions, handled the materials and got involved in the demonstrations. The demonstrations and displays educated the general public on the rich cultural heritage of traditional Hawaiian society, and reassured them that the Hawaiian culture is still alive and being taught to succeeding generations. The Hawaiians of the future will continue to be enriched by the gift of knowledge imparted to them by their

The art of the ancient people of Hawai'i is perpetuated through the skillful hands of Ethelreda Kahalewai (*right*) sewing a feather *lei*. Other practitioners of distinctive Hawaiian crafts are (*counterclockwise*) Deborah Kepola Kakalia quilting, Moana Espinda weaving coconut leaves, and Duncan Ka'ohu Seto working on *lauhala*. (OHA photo by Deborah Ward)

72

'ONIPA'A
FIVE DAYS
IN THE
HISTORY
OF THE
HAWAIIAN
NATION

1893-1993

ancestors through the centuries.

On the grounds of the Mission Houses Museum across the street, the Hawaiian Entrepreneurs Fair drew thousands of people to view the wares being offered by more than 30 entrepreneurs. Items sold ranged from Hawaiian theme T-shirts to paddles for outrigger canoeing to clothing, jewelry, *lomi* sticks, books, and, of course, food.

Certainly one of the most popular items being sold was the official centennial observance T-shirt designed by committee member Momi Cazimero. With the likeness of Queen Lili'uokalani emblazoned on purple, white, or black shirts, this souvenir attracted people in lines two and three deep winding around the museum and down King Street. The shirts were entirely sold out and orders were taken for future delivery.

The food vendors ran out of food after serving hundreds of Hawaiian plate lunches, stew, shave ice, soda, and more. Many other vendors also sold out of their products during the day, saying that this was without a doubt the best fair in which they had ever participated.

The Mission Houses Museum prepared a special Hawaiian quilt exhibit for the event which was viewed by hundreds of people. Museum Executive Director Deborah Pope was so overwhelmed by the success and goodwill of the fair, that she offered the 'Onipa'a Committee the use of the site for another such event. Although the Committee offered to give the Museum a portion of the booth fees for the restoration of the grounds, stress on the facilities, and for cleanup, the Museum refused the payment, saying the use of their grounds and facilities was a gift to the Hawaiian people.

The craft fair on the grounds of the Mission Houses Museum provided dozens of Hawaiian entrepreneurs with an opportunity to present their products while commemorating the 100th anniversary of the overthrow of the Hawaiian monarchy. (Deborah Pope photo)

Long lines of people waiting to purchase the official 'Onipa'a shirt crowd the sidewalks around the museum as many vendors sell out their inventories during the day. (Deborah Pope photo)

'Onipa'a Chair
Tungpalan and Dr.
Kekuni Blaisdell,
Hawaiian sovereignty
advocate of the organiza-
tion Ka Pākaukau, share
their *mana'o* as work on
the *ahu* begins. (Eliza-
beth Pa Martin photo)

'ONIPA'A
FIVE DAYS
IN THE
HISTORY
OF THE
HAWAIIAN
NATION

1893-1993

Emotions were overflowing during the centennial activities as Hawaiians from all walks of life felt
the pride of their nation reunited. 'Onipa'a Chair Tungpalan here embraces Dr. Kekuni Blaisdell as
James Bartels, curator of 'Iolani Palace, looks on. (Elizabeth Pa Martin photo)

The *ahu* slowly grows as Palikapu o Kamohoaliʻi Dedman (*left*) waits for more *pōhaku*. This sacred altar was constructed as a symbol of the intent to heal the wounds between the *makaʻāinana* and the *aliʻi* and upon completion became a comfortable meeting place for many Hawaiian groups. (Elizabeth Paʻ Martin photo)

Standing in black and white *kīhei* is Hawaiian spiritual leader, the late Parley Kanakaʻole, who watches as spiritual offerings are presented at the *ahu* or altar that was erected on ʻIolani Palace grounds. (Elizabeth Paʻ Martin photo)

Robert Kalanihiapo Wilcox (played by Kīhei Soli Nīheu) delivers an emotional plea that "We must stand together! We must stand tall, proud and steadfast!" Thousands in the audience responded with an outpouring of cheers. (Elizabeth Pa Martin photo)

'ONIPA'A
FIVE DAYS
IN THE
HISTORY
OF THE
HAWAIIAN
NATION

1893-1993

William White (played by Frank Nobriga), a newspaper publisher and member of the Legislature of the Hawaiian Kingdom, rallies all true royalists behind Queen Lili'uokalani, warning them that a "serpent is in the garden." (Elizabeth Pa Martin photo)

Speaking for the annexationists, R. J. Green (played by Ben Berman) rails against the Queen. (Elizabeth Pa Martin photo)

Pōkā Laenui of the Hawaiian Broadcast Company conducts a "living history" interview with supporters of Queen Liliʻuokalani, Herman Widemann (played by Niklaus Schweizer) and his wife Haʻaheo Widemann (played by Alexis Lopez), regarding the crisis facing the monarchy. In a style reminiscent of the old radio show, "I Can Hear It Now," the historical re-enactments were broadcast live over Hawaiʻi Public Radio. (Elizabeth Pa Martin photo)

'ONIPA'A
FIVE DAYS
IN THE
HISTORY
OF THE
HAWAIIAN
NATION

1893-1993

As a light rain fell upon the grounds of 'Iolani Palace, The Royal Hawaiian Band performed a concert just as it did 100 years earlier on the evening of January 16, 1893. Before the concert, the sound of troops marching through Honolulu streets was re-created in remembrance of the illegal invasion of Hawai'i by military personnel of the *U.S.S. Boston*. (*Advertiser* photo by Gregory Yamamoto)

SKYGATE CONCERT: A MUSICAL
TRIBUTE TO QUEEN LILIʻUOKALANI

The music of the Hawaiian people has always been more than entertainment. Their songs, chants, and dances have been a means of passing through the generations the history, genealogy and the spiritual lessons of what it means to be Hawaiian. Thus the musical tribute to Queen Liliʻuokalani presented at the Skygate Concert on Saturday afternoon was not only to honor Hawaiʻi's beloved *aliʻi*, but also to allow the thousands in attendance to experience those intangible feelings expressed through music.

On the vast expanse of lawn between City Hall and the City Municipal Building, the crowds listened. They brought their mats, lawn chairs, coolers with refreshments, and umbrellas for shade, and were uplifted by the wealth of talent shared by award-winning musicians, vocalists, chanters, and *hula* dancers. The audience was composed of entire families from *kūpuna* to *kamaliʻi*. The majority were of Hawaiian ancestry, but people of all ethnic backgrounds joined this musical tribute to Hawaiʻi's last monarch.

During the early months of preparation for the concert, a long list of Hawaiʻi's entertainers was asked if they would be willing to offer their time and talent to the centennial observance. Without exception, they said "yes!" Even those already committed to other events rearranged their schedules to participate. Mike Kelly, general manager of KCCN radio, and his staff were pressed into service to gather and schedule each group or individual. Omar the Tent Man supplied the stage and the tents for changing. Woody Barboza provided the staging and the sound systems, while Nā Pualei O Likolehua performed and served as the hostesses.

Songs and dances in tribute to Queen Liliʻuokalani were performed that day as well as music she had written herself. A prolific and sensitive composer, the Queen left a musical legacy which includes over 165 songs. Many of these, like "The Queen's Prayer" and "Aloha ʻOe," are still popular. The range of musical selections was impressive as each group performed those numbers which have become popular standards in their repertoire.

The crowds were overwhelmingly responsive to all the entertainers and *hālau hula* that appeared that day. The lineup was a Who's Who of modern Hawaiian music: Olomana, the Brothers Cazimero, the Mākaha Sons of Niʻihau with Lydia Kauakāhi's Hālau Kahanuola, Moe Keale, Kawai Cockett, Keʻalohi with Leimomi Ho's Kealiʻi Kaʻapunihonua Keʻena Aʻo Hula, Henry Kapono, Loyal Garner and her niece Piʻilani Smith, Stan Nakasone, Bill Kaʻiwa, Owana Salazar, Kaʻau Crater Boys, Haʻaheo, Joe Tassill and Liko Martin, and Leon Siu.

Other *hālau* were: Pua Aliʻi ʻIlima-*Kumu Hula* Victoria Holt Takamine, Hālau Mōhala ʻIlima-*Kumu Hula* Māpuana de Silva, Hālau Nā Mamo O Puʻuanahulu-*Kumu Hula* William "Sonny" Ching, Kawailiʻulā-*Kumu Hula* Chinky Māhoe, Pūpūkāhi I Ke Alo O Nā Pua-instructor Michael Casupang, Hālau Ke Kapa Maile-*Kumu Hula* Randy Ngum, the Lehua Dance Company-*Kumu Hula* Kaulana Kasparovitch, and Keʻalohilohi O Ka Ua Laʻi Lani, He Hālau Hula-*Kumu Hula* Aaron Yacapin.

As the concert continued into the late afternoon, on the other side of the Capitol district near the Old Federal Building, other events evoked memories of the invasion of the Kingdom of Hawaiʻi, and the ramifications of that illegal action on the sovereignty of the land.

'ONIPAʻA
FIVE DAYS
IN THE
HISTORY
OF THE
HAWAIIAN
NATION

1893-1993

NĀ KOA WARRIORS KA LĀHUI HAWAI'I
AND LANDING OF THE U.S. TROOPS

On the afternoon of January 16, 1893, the 162 U.S. soldiers arrived within a block of 'Iolani Palace. Their presence was a major factor in the overthrow of the Hawaiian monarchy. This illegal invasion of a sovereign kingdom was vigorously protested by Queen Lili'uokalani, who recognized the presence of these troops as blatant support for the Committee of Public Safety. The troops were bivouacked at Arion Hall, today the location of the Old Federal Building Post Office and Customs House.

One hundred years later, the Nā Koa warriors of Ka Lāhui Hawai'i stood peacefully in front of the Old Federal Building, close to the location where the troops were stationed in 1893. Dressed in ceremonial attire and bearing wooden spears, the Nā Koa took a spiritual approach to reverse the injustice which occurred 100 years ago. Chants for spiritual cleansing and for spiritual guidance toward achieving sovereignty were performed.

Not long after this, public rallies were held across the street at the Coronation Pavilion as the "living history" program re-created the public rallies which had aroused the people of Honolulu a century earlier. The crowds on the Palace grounds grew during the day, in the same way that concerned citizens of 1893 had crowded the public meetings of both the Committee of Public Safety and the Royalists. As the volatile and threatening speeches of those supporting the overthrow of the Queen were delivered, the audience was reminded that while the words of history could be condemned as inflammatory, the actors were only performing those sentiments in a portrayal of the past.

The Royalists meeting that followed was marked by outpourings of patriotic emotion for Queen Lili'uokalani and Hawaiian independence. The highlight came as Kīhei Soli Nīheu playing Robert Kalanihiapo Wilcox, tearfully called out to the teeming crowd, "We must stand together! We must

stand tall, proud and steadfast! We must firmly stand together as one people because of that which binds us together! We love our Kingdom! We love our Queen! We love the land that gave us birth!" The cry brought thousands to their feet in a thundering ovation. At that moment, a light shower fell upon the crowd.

The evening was filled with a new sound as beating drums, marching feet and the barking commands of an officer in charge approached from the harbor. As the movement of "U.S. troops" grew louder, the grounds of the Palace were filled with the sound of an intruding, threatening presence. Although the re-creation of the invasion of the island was done with sound alone, the effect was more chilling and sorrowful than if it had been staged with actors.

After the exciting re-creation of the landing and marching of the troops, the Royal Hawaiian Band performed a concert from the Coronation Bandstand. In the early evening of January 16, 1893, the Royal Hawaiian Band, under the direction of Bandmaster Henri Berger, had also given a public concert across the street from 'Iolani Palace at the Hawaiian Hotel. "Perfect quietness reigned through the city," Marshal Charles Wilson later remarked, "there being a band concert at the hotel, which was attended by a large and peaceable crowd, as usual." Now, exactly 100 years later, the Royal Hawaiian Band, under the direction of Bandmaster Aaron Mahi, repeated that performance.

Crowds listened with affection just as Queen Lili'uokalani did on the last evening of her reign. Another light rain passed through the crowd, as if the sky above Honolulu was filled with sadness.

Pōkā Laenui of the Hawaiian Broadcast Company, which had been broadcasting all of the "living history" drama live over Hawai'i Public Radio, moved through the audience, asking the historic characters to describe the scene of the marching troops. Over radio, the combination of the background sound and historic interviews produced an uncanny sense of reality. When the marching of the troops finally came to a halt, the large audience and costumed role-players instinctively joined hands and sang "Hawai'i Pono'i."

As the day came to a close, downtown Honolulu slowly emptied. Exhausted vendors at the grounds of the Mission Houses Museum packed up their equipment and headed home. Patrons with their purchases drifted off with a new awareness of the ancient and contemporary skill of the Hawaiians. Across the street at Skygate, darkness had finally brought the concert to an end, although the delighted and enthusiastic audience would have gladly stayed and enjoyed the event well into the night. The audience and performers left with the knowledge that they had all been part of an historical moment. Filled with a love for their Queen, they had honored her in a fashion which she would have embraced.

Where the U.S. troops had spent the night on January 16, 1893, Nā Koa stood watch over the kūpuna of Ka Lāhui Hawai'i, as they held a vigil until midnight. Torches burned into the night, their melancholy yellow glow fading as the mournful day of January 17 began to dawn.

'ONIPA'A
FIVE DAYS
IN THE
HISTORY
OF THE
HAWAIIAN
NATION

1893-1993

CHAPTER SEVEN

January 17, 1893:
The Overthrow of the Hawaiian Kingdom

By an act of war, committed with the participation of a diplomatic representative of the United States and without authority of Congress, the Government of a feeble but friendly and confiding people has been overthrown. A substantial wrong has thus been done which a due regard for our national character as well as the rights of the injured people requires we should endeavor to repair.

Grover Cleveland
U.S. President
December 18, 1893

'ONIPA'A
FIVE DAYS
IN THE
HISTORY
OF THE
HAWAIIAN
NATION

1893-1993

The U.S. military occupa-
tion of Hawai'i becomes
more evident on January
17, 1893 as troops pose
for the photographer in
front of Ali'iōlani Hale.
(Bishop Museum photo)

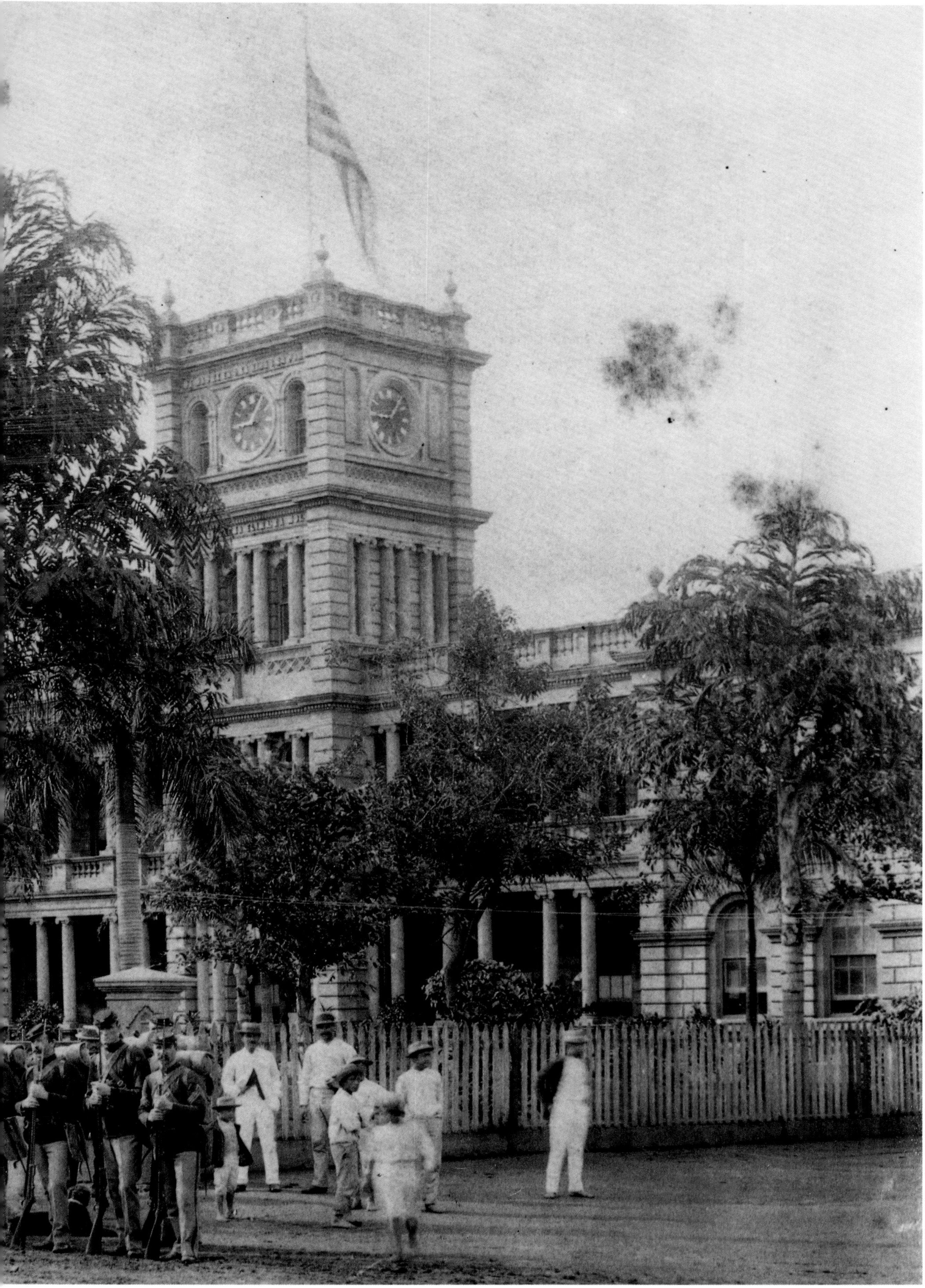

"Tuesday morning, the town is very quiet," said John Lot Kaulukou, a supporter of the Queen, in recalling January 17, 1893, the single most tragic day in the history of the Hawaiian nation. "We never had any idea of a revolution or disturbance."

The *Ka Leo O Ka Lāhui* newspaper carried a notice advising its Hawaiian readers to "conduct themselves peacefully, not to cause any unrest, or do anything that might provoke a riot." A news article in the Hawaiian language paper reported that, while an American man-of-war should not land its troops without the knowledge of the Hawaiian government, the U.S. minister had in fact ordered the sailors of the *U.S.S. Boston* deployed. "It would appear that this is a strong-arm action on his part, and if and when the American government investigates fully the truth of his actions, his superiors will decide that he has made the wrong decision." The newspaper also carried a report that the British and French governments were preparing to send warships to support Queen Liliʻuokalani. "Therefore, O commoners, we who love Queen Liliʻuokalani, observe the command of our ruling Chief and do as she has instructed us: 'Be patient and wait quietly.' Therefore, don't despair or protest. It is the Lord who shall give us help."

Kaulukou was at the Police Headquarters, also called the Station House, on Merchant Street, where Marshal Charles Wilson stood by the Cabinet and the Queen's Gatling guns. Capt. Samuel Nowlein, commander of the Queen's troops and Household Guard, prepared to defend ʻIolani Palace and the royal barracks.

Professor William Alexander said volunteers in the annexationist camp were tense but believed the Queen's supporters were "panic-stricken and divided among themselves." At 9:00 a.m., banker and former Cabinet member Samuel Damon visited the Queen to tell her he had been asked to join a revolutionary council. Liliʻuokalani suggested he join. "I had no idea that they intended to

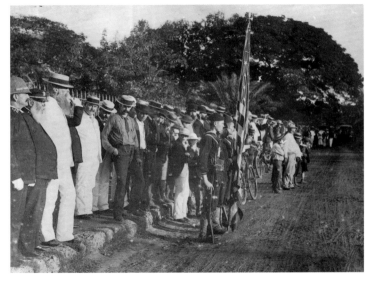

ʻONIPAʻA
FIVE DAYS
IN THE
HISTORY
OF THE
HAWAIIAN
NATION

1893-1993

On January 17, 1893, Sanford B. Dole, President of the Provisional Government (*third from the left*), watches military troops from the *U.S.S. Boston*, consisting of three companies of sailors, an artillery battery, and a Marine company parade down King Street. To his right, Captain Gilbert C. Wiltse looks on as troops invade Honolulu. (Hawaiʻi State Archives photo)

(Adapted from "Day by Day Account of the 1893 Overthrow," *Honolulu Advertiser*, by Stu Glauberman. The original Glauberman article ends on January 17, 1893. The description of the events beginning with the surrender of the Royal Guard on January 18, 1893 through 1959 statehood is original material that has been included to provide a fuller understanding of the aftermath of the overthrow of the Hawaiian monarchy.)

ARMY OF HAWAII
1893
FIRST COMPANY, SHARPSHOOTERS

Identification number of each on the picture, reading from top left to right, and so on down the line:

1 L.L. La Pierre	8 J. B. Castle	15 F. Hustace
2 J. Armstrong	9 A. B. Wood	16 John Farnsworth
3 M. N. Sanders	10 Dan Lyons	17 C.J. Campbell
4 Archie Gilfillan	11 W.F. Dillingham	18 C.J. Wall
5 Wm. Ross	12 John Grace	19 J. Whitney
6 Jos. Marsden	13 W.T. Monsarrat	20 J. D. McVeigh
7 G. Schuman	14 F. Clifford	21 John Cassidy

22 N.B. Emerson	29 W. J. Forbes	36 F. L. Leslie
23 W.H. Wilkinson	30 J. B. Gibson	37 J. A. McCandless
24 C. Johnson	31 John F. Scott	38 O. E. Wall
25 F. A. Hosmer	32 J. A. Magoon	39 C. A. Rice
26 J. L. McLean	33 J. S. Emerson	40 A. W. Keech
27 R. L. Warson	34 M. Philp	41 F. B. Damon
28 E. A. Murphy	35 L.L. McCandless	42 Allen Judd

43 F. S. Dodge	50 Rev. H.W. Peck
44 *Capt.* John Kidwell	*Not in the picture:*
45 W. E. Wall	D. W. Corbett
46 W. A. Wall	Rev. O.P. Emerson
47 Wm. McCandless	F. W. McChesney
48 J.S. McCandless	J.M. McChesney
49 J. S. Martin	A.E. Nichol
	E.C. Winston

Supporters of the Provisional Government organized themselves as the Army of Hawai'i and helped carry out the overthrow of the Queen. (Bishop Museum photo)

On January 18, 1893, Captain Samuel Nowlein (*second from the right*) listens as the newly-appointed Provisional Government military chief, Col. John H. Soper (*in derby*) dismisses the Queen's Royal Guard. (Hawai'i State Archives photo)

88

'ONIPA'A
FIVE DAYS
IN THE
HISTORY
OF THE
HAWAIIAN
NATION

1893-1993

Troops of the Provisional Government barricade the entrances to 'Iolani Palace in the aftermath of the overthrow of the Hawaiian Monarchy. (Hawai'i State Archives photo)

establish a new Government," she said.

Many Hawaiian citizens spent the day "down the city," as did the ex-revolutionary Robert Wilcox. "People were running about—all curious about seeing the *Boston*'s men on shore," he said. Wilcox said committee members were working hard to enlist men in the volunteer army forming among businessmen and tradesmen. According to Dr. Francis Day, "We understood that at a given signal, those who were in favor of the movement were to meet at the Honolulu Rifles Armory, with arms, and proceed upon the Government Building."

At 1:00 p.m., sugar planters' executive P.C. Jones got a telephone call, summoning him to Smith's law offices to join the others who had agreed to be executives and advisers in a new government. They had worked out a plan for a provisional government to maintain the peace until annexation to the United States. Sanford Dole had resigned as a judge earlier that morning to become chairman of the four-man executive committee that would proclaim and run the temporary government. Dole formally accepted the presidency at William O. Smith's law office. Members of the executive council of the provisional government were James A. King, Sanford B. Dole, William O. Smith and Peter C. Jones.

Aware that the annexationists planned to depose the Queen that day, the Queen's Cabinet drove up Nu'uanu Avenue to see U.S. Minister John Stevens at the Legation. "After talking with him quite a while," said Minister John Colburn, "he gave us no definite answer and we left him and returned to the Police Station to make our headquarters there, and to write Mr. Stevens about his position."

Meanwhile Dole, with his executives and advisers, planned to proclaim the new government at Ali'iōlani Hale at 3:00 p.m. So as not to attract attention, they left at 2:40 p.m. and split up, with most walking up Merchant Street, and some taking Queen Street.

As they left the office, a pistol shot was heard from Hall's Corner, a block away on King Street, and a crowd gathered there. Earlier, a cart driven by annexationists had left the E.O. Hall & Sons store

Sandbags, rifles and soldiers block the side entrances to the Palace, which will be renamed the Executive Building. Many of the royal furnishings and treasures of the Hawaiian Monarchy will be looted or auctioned off by the new occupants. (Bishop Museum photo)

90

'ONIPA'A
FIVE DAYS
IN THE
HISTORY
OF THE
HAWAIIAN
NATION

1893-1993

Immediately after the overthrow of Queen Lili'uokalani, an Annexation Commission hurried to Washington, D.C., to negotiate with U.S. President Benjamin Harrison for the U.S. acquisition of the islands. Lorrin A. Thurston, the driving force behind the annexation scheme, is flanked by the other members of the Annexation Commis-sion. Left to Right: William C. Wilder, Joseph Marsden, Charles L. Carter (*standing*), Lorrin A. Thurston, Dr. John Mott-Smith (not a commission member) and William R. Castle. President Harrison ended his term of office in early 1893 before annexation could be completed. (Bishop Museum photo)

After his inauguration, U.S. President Grover Cleveland sent Commis-sioner James Blount (pictured here with his wife Eugenie W. Blount) to Hawai'i to conduct a thorough investigation of the events surround-ing the insurrection and overthrow of the Hawaiian Monarchy on January 17, 1893. The Blount Report con-demned the activities of U.S. Minister Stevens during the overthrow as an abuse of his author-ity. (Bishop Museum photo)

loaded with arms and ammunition. A Hawaiian policeman named Leialoha, who had been watching the store, tried to stop the wagon. The annexationists' ordnance officer drew his revolver and shot the unarmed policeman in the shoulder.

Unable to complete their schemes for annexation, the Provisional Government declared itself the Republic of Hawai'i on July 4, 1894, with Sanford B. Dole (*center, white beard*) elected president. (Hawai'i State Archives photo)

"This occurrence brought the people's excitement up to fire heat," said Marshal Wilson. The incident served as a signal both to the annexationists, who hurried to the Beretania Street Armory, and to Hawaiians, who flocked to the Station House on Merchant Street.

When Dole and the members of his government-to-be arrived at Ali'iōlani Hale to fulfill their mission, scarcely anyone was around. "With the exception of the clerks of the different departments, the Government Building was deserted," Dole said. When he looked around for signs of armed volunteers to protect him and the others, Dole found only one volunteer present. Likewise, the government's force was represented by one man, without any back-up force.

Inside the building, Judge Henry Cooper, Dole's vice chairman, promptly began reading the proclamation. Cooper's hand shook as he read. At first, only half a dozen spectators were present.

"It took just about 10 minutes [to read] and in that time, our forces, our men, were coming in from the Armory," said Jones. Before long, according to Jones, the armed force had grown to between 150 and 200 men. They stood in formation at the building's main entrance. Royalist Fred Wundenberg said he could see the U.S. troops in their temporary quarters 100 yards away. They "appeared to be under arms and were evidently ready for any emergency."

At 3:00 that afternoon, Chairman Dole and his Cabinet, with the help of two government clerks, took over the offices of the Interior Ministry. "We commenced to formulate our plans and get ourselves into working order," said Samuel Damon, the Queen's confidant who was now an adviser to the provisional government. Dole then dashed off a letter notifying American Minister John Stevens and other diplomats that a provisional government was in possession of the government building and the archives.

About 75 yards away, U.S. sailors and Marines of the *Boston* lounged about the yard of Arion Hall. Their muskets were stacked. Only two sentries were armed.

Following the proclamation of the new government, a former finance minister, J.S. Walker, went across to the Palace to tell the Queen it was his painful duty to inform her she must abdicate. She told Walker she had no intention of doing so.

At the Station House, Marshal Charles Wilson asked the Cabinet for permission to send his armed forces to surround the insurrectionists at Ali'iōlani Hale "and shoot them down, as they were only a handful."

U.S. Navy Lt. Lucien Young visited Dole at the government building on behalf of the U.S. naval commander, Capt. Gilbert Wiltse, to determine the extent of provisional government control. An aide to Minister Stevens went along. When Dole conceded he did not control the Station House or the Barracks, Young replied, "If you have not charge of the government, I am requested to inform you that we can have nothing to do with you."

At the Station House, loyalist John Lot Kaulukou waited with other Hawaiians and foreigners who were prepared to fight. The Queen's government had 600 men with rifles and 30,000 rounds of

After an aborted attempt to restore the Hawaiian Monarchy in January 1895 under the leadership of Samuel Nowlein, Robert Wilcox and hundreds of Royalists, Lili'uokalani was arrested at her home at Washington Place. Here, the Queen is escorted up the back steps of the 'Iolani Palace under armed guard. (Hawai'i State Archives photo)

'ONIPA'A
FIVE DAYS
IN THE
HISTORY
OF THE
HAWAIIAN
NATION

1893-1993

The trial of Queen Lili'uokalani for "misprision of treason," the failure to disclose knowledge of an act of treason to the appropriate officials, was an attempt by the Republic to publicly humiliate the Queen. In this sketch from the *San Francisco Examiner* of February 16, 1895, attorney Paul Neumann defends her before a military tribunal. She was convicted of the charge and served eight months under house arrest in her own palace. (Hawai'i State Archives photo)

ammunition, eight brass field cannons and two Gatling guns.

At about 2:45 p.m., the Queen's ministers had sent Noble Charles L. Hopkins with a protest note to Stevens, asking whether the United States was going to recognize the provisional government made up of "certain treasonable persons [who] at present occupy the Government building."

"We thought before Hopkins went up there that Mr. Stevens was in favor of Her Majesty's government," Kaulukou said. But the mood changed when Hopkins returned about an hour later with Stevens' reply — the Queen's ministers were no longer ministers because Stevens had recognized the Provisional Government. "For that reason, we could not do anything, because we did not want to fight with the United States government," Kaulukou said.

About 4:00 o'clock, the Queen's ministers sent for the annexationists to come to the Station House. "We refused to go, and assured them if they would come up and interview us, we would talk over this situation," said Provisional Government executive committee member Peter Jones.

Provisional Government advisory council members Crister Bolte and Samuel Damon went to the Station House to induce the Queen's supporters to give up. As Bolte put it, "It would be useless shedding of blood if we got into a fight over this thing." Marshal Wilson refused to surrender without written orders approved by the Queen.

While the talks went on, pro-annexationist volunteers were afraid of what might happen. "For several hours, it looked to us as if a bloody contest, and perhaps a siege, would be necessary," said Professor William Alexander.

At about 6:00 p.m., all four of the Queen's ministers got into a pair of hacks and returned with Bolte and Damon to talk to Dole. "They agreed to desist, but said they must go to the Queen and get her to confer with them," Damon said. Damon

(Facing page) One of the Royalists arrested, convicted and sentenced of "misprision of treason" was Prince Jonah Kūhiō Kalaniana'ole, shown here wearing the stripes of a common criminal. (Hawai'i State Archives photo)

On August 12, 1898, American Blue Jackets and Marines from the *U.S.S. Philadelphia* landed at Honolulu Harbor to take part in the Annexation Day ceremonies at ʻIolani Palace. (Hawaiʻi State Archives photo)

94

'ONIPA'A
FIVE DAYS
IN THE
HISTORY
OF THE
HAWAIIAN
NATION

1893-1993

Although in 1897 over 29,000 Hawaiians signed a petition voicing their opposition to annexation and requesting the issue be submitted to a vote throughout the islands, the United States and the ruling leaders of the Republic pushed the measure through in 1898 without a plebiscite. With the final lowering of the Hawaiian flag, the will of the majority and the self-determination of the nation had been subverted. (Bishop Museum photo)

went with them to the Palace, where the Queen waited in the Blue Room.

Each recommended surrender, saying resistance would provoke bloodshed and that the forces arrayed against the Queen would be too strong to overcome. "It was the Queen's idea that she could surrender pending a settlement at Washington, and it was on that condition that she gave up," Damon said. Faced with these arguments, the Queen agreed to yield and issued a carefully worded note of protest:

"I, Lili'uokalani, by the Grace of God and under the Constitution of the Kingdom, Queen, do hereby solemnly protest against any and all acts done against myself and the constitutional government of the Hawaiian Kingdom by certain persons claiming to have established a provisional government of and for this Kingdom.

"That I yield to the superior force of the United States of America, whose minister plenipotentiary, His Excellence John L. Stevens, has caused United States troops to be landed at Honolulu and declared that he would support the said provisional government.

"Now, to avoid any collision of armed forces and perhaps the loss of life, I do under this protest, and impelled by said force, yield my authority until such time as the Government of the United States shall, upon the facts being presented to it, undo the action of its representatives and reinstate me in the authority which I claim as the constitutional sovereign of the Hawaiian Islands."

The sun was setting when Finance Minister William Cornwell delivered the Queen's written note to Dole, who received it and dated it on the back.

Attorney General Arthur Peterson was dispatched to instruct Wilson to deliver up the police station and O'ahu prison to the "so-called" provisional government.

"That wound up the whole affair," said Damon.

"I went home and got dinner," said Bolte. "I was home about 7 o'clock."

That evening, Dole signed two proclamations, one urging supporters to furnish the new government with arms and ammunition, the other declaring martial law and suspending the writ of habeas corpus.

The volunteers at the Station House were dejected. "We could have gone up there and cleaned those soldiers of the provisional government out in 15 or 20 minutes," Kaulukou said. "We had everything ready to go and fight." After being disarmed by Marshal Wilson, the Queen's supporters gave three hearty cheers and dispersed quietly.

Samuel Nowlein, the hold-out commander of the Queen's Royal Guard, assembled his unit in the courtyard of 'Iolani Barracks on the morning of Wednesday, January 18, 1893, two days after the armed invasion of the sovereign nation of Hawai'i. There the Royal Guard were dismissed by Col. John H. Soper, the newly appointed Provisional Government military chief. After taking away their arms, Col. Soper paid each man a stipend through the end of the month. Every facet of the Hawaiian monarchy that had ruled the islands for over 100 years was being dismantled.

The Provisional Government quickly set up its own forces at 'Iolani Palace, which they renamed the Executive Building. By the first week of February, artillery men flanked by cannons were prepared to go to battle should the citizens loyal to the lawful government of Hawai'i fight for its return.

In Washington, D.C., news of the insurrection in Hawai'i and the involvement of U.S. Minister Stevens and troops of the *U.S.S. Boston* concerned President Grover Cleveland and the United States Congress. To determine what actually took place in the islands, Congressman James Blount was sent to Hawai'i to conduct an investigation. While conducting interviews of the participants in the events surrounding the overthrow of the monarchy, Commissioner Blount was informed by the Queen's Minister, Arthur P. Peterson, that U.S. Minister Stevens had not only refused to come to the aid of the Queen's government, but said that if the insurgents

'ONIPA'A
FIVE DAYS
IN THE
HISTORY
OF THE
HAWAIIAN
NATION

1893-1993

The flag of the Hawaiian nation is lowered for the last time from 'Iolani Palace on August 12, 1898, Annexation Day. (Bishop Museum photo)

were attacked and arrested by the Queen's forces, the United States troops would intervene. Peterson further stated that Stevens said if responsible citizens established a provisional government, he would recognize and support it. Stevens later denied these accusations, saying that there was no mention of using troops to support those opposing the Queen.

The report of this presidential investigation of the events surrounding the insurrection and overthrow of January 17, 1893 found otherwise, concluding that the United States diplomatic and military representatives had abused their authority and were responsible for the change in government.

In his message to Congress on December 18, 1893, President Grover Cleveland reported fully and accurately on the illegal acts of the conspirators. He described the event as an "act of war, committed with the participation of a diplomatic representative of the United States and without the authority of Congress." He acknowledged that by such acts the government of a peaceful and friendly people was overthrown. President Cleveland further concluded that a "substantial wrong has thus been done which a due regard for our national character as well as the rights of the injured people requires that we should endeavor to repair." Minister Stevens was therefore recalled from his diplomatic post by President Cleveland. Captain Wiltse was disciplined and forced to resign his commission.

The Provisional Government protested President Cleveland's call for the restoration of the monarchy. They continued to hold power and pursued annexation to the United States, successfully lobbying the Committee on Foreign Relations of the Senate to conduct a new investigation into the events surrounding the overthrow of the monarchy. The Committee and its chairman, Senator John Morgan, conducted hearings in Washington, D. C., from December 27, 1893 through February 26, 1894. At the hearings, members of the Provisional Government justified the actions of the United States Minister and recommended annexation of Hawai'i. Although the Provisional Government obscured the role of the United States in the illegal overthrow of

Queen Lili'uokalani sits in Washington Place surrounded by family, nobles, and other loyalists who refused to attend the annexation ceremony and the raising of the flag of the United States. (Bishop Museum photo)

the Hawaiian monarchy, it was unable to rally the support of the two-thirds of the Senate needed to ratify a treaty of annexation.

Frustrated in its attempts to annex the islands to the United States, on July 4, 1894, the Provisional Government declared itself the Republic of Hawai'i and Sanford B. Dole was elected its president. Loyalty oaths were required for participation in the new government. A coalition of Hawaiians led by Samuel Nowlein and Robert Wilcox, opposed to the Republic and supported by scores of non-Hawaiians still loyal to the Queen, rebelled and attempted an overthrow of the illegal government in January 1895. Over 100 individuals including Nowlein, Wilcox, Prince Kūhiō and Liliʻuokalani were arrested by the Republic's National Guard and "Citizen Guards."

The act of trying and sentencing the Queen was a strategic maneuver to discourage the Royalists. Unable to charge the Queen with treason, the Republic of Hawaiʻi accused her of "misprision of treason," the failure to disclose knowledge of an act of treason to the appropriate officials. Despite a strong defense by her attorney Paul Neumann, the Queen was convicted and sentenced to five years' hard labor. She actually served a humiliating eight-month house arrest, confined to a second-floor suite in her former palace.

During her imprisonment, the Queen was told by Neumann that she and six other loyalists were scheduled to be shot unless she abdicated. She replied that she was not afraid of dying. The Queen wrote later, "For myself, I would have chosen death rather than to have signed it [the document asserting her complicity]; but it was represented to me that by my signing this paper all the persons who had been arrested, all my people now in trouble by reason of their love and loyalty towards me, would be immediately released." Eventually all the Royalists were pardoned. The Queen was the last prisoner to be released.

One of the men who was imprisoned for his heroic defiance of the Republic of Hawaiʻi was Prince Jonah Kūhiō Kalanianaʻole, an heir to the Kingdom, and a lineal descendant of Kaumualiʻi, the last ruling chief of Kauaʻi. Kūhiō's alleged crime was to side with his cousin, Queen Liliʻuokalani, during the Royalist uprising. He was sentenced as a criminal to a year of hard labor spent repairing the masonry on the prison walls. Later, in the second Territorial election of 1902, Prince Kūhiō successfully ran for the Congressional delegate's seat and was re-elected nine times by his loyal constituency. He was a primary force behind the establishment of the Hawaiian Homes Commission Act of 1920.

The Queen's account of what had taken place would have been buried in the rewriting of history

that began immediately after the overthrow if she had not written *Hawaiʻi's Story by Hawaiʻi's Queen* in 1898. In it, she told how her kingdom had been stolen. She called upon Americans to listen to the cries of her downtrodden people and recognize that "their form of government is as dear to them as yours is precious to you. Quite as warmly as you love your country, so they love theirs." To those who would ask why she did not use the force of arms to repel the invaders, her explanation revealed the depth of her love for all her subjects, of whatever race:

> *"To prevent the shedding of the blood of my people, natives and foreigners alike. I opposed armed interference and quietly yielded to the armed forces brought against my Throne, and submitted to the arbitrament of the government of the United States the decision of my rights, and those of the Hawaiian people. Since then, as is well known to all, I have pursued the path of peace and diplomatic discussion, and not that of internal strife."*

The Hawaiian people also opposed American annexation through their songs. "Kaulana Nā Pua," written in 1893 by Ellen Wright Prendergast, was directly inspired by members of the Royal Hawaiian Band who had expressed their opposition to the islands being taken over by the Provisional Government. According to Ethel M. Damon, the composer's daughter, on an afternoon in January 1893, Ellen Prendergast sat in her garden with her guitar close at hand. She was visited by members of the Royal Hawaiian Band who were on strike. Proclaiming their allegiance to Queen Liliʻuokalani, they declared that they would not follow the new government nor would they sign the *haole's* loyalty oath. They stated that they would rather eat stones, the mystic food of their native land, and asked Prendergast to compose a song of rebellion. This *"Mele ʻAi Pōhaku,"* Stone-Eating Song, became a well-loved melody among Hawaiians, despite the new government's attempts to ban its being played.

ʻONIPAʻA
FIVE DAYS
IN THE
HISTORY
OF THE
HAWAIIAN
NATION

1893-1993

KAULANA NĀ PUA

Kaulana nā pua a'o Hawai'i
Kūpa'a ma hope o ka 'āina
Hiki mai ka 'elele o ka loko 'ino
Palapala 'ānunu me ka pākaha.

Pane mai Hawai'i moku o Keawe.
Kōkua nā hono a'o Pi'ilani.
Kāko'o mai Kaua'i o Mano
Pau pū me ke one Kākuhihewa.

'A'ole a'e kau i ka pūlima
Ma luna o ka pepa o ka 'enemi
Ho'ohui 'āina kū'ai hewa
I ka pono sivila a'o ke kanaka.

'A'ole mākou a'e minamina
I ka pu'ukālā a ke aupuni.
Ua lawa mākou i ka pōhaku,
I ka 'ai kamaha'o o ka 'āina.

Ma hope mākou o Lili'u-lani
A loa'a ē ka pono a ka 'āina.
(*A kau hou 'ia e ke kalaunu*)
Ha'ina 'ia mai ana ka puana
Ka po'e i aloha i ka 'āina.

FAMOUS ARE THE FLOWERS

Famous are the children of Hawai'i
Ever loyal to the land
When the evil-hearted messenger comes
With his greedy document of extortion.

Hawai'i, land of Keawe answers.
Pi'ilani's bays help.
Mano's Kaua'i lends support
And so do the sands of Kākuhihewa.

No one will fix a signature
To the paper of the enemy
With its sin of annexation
And sale of native civil rights.

We do not value
The government's sums of money.
We are satisfied with the stones,
Astonishing food of the land.

We back Lili'u-lani
Who has won the rights of the land.
(She will be crowned again)
Tell the story
Of the people who love their land.

© <u>Nā Mele o Hawai'i</u>
By Noelani Māhoe
Written by:
Ellen Wright Prendergast

'ONIPA'A
FIVE DAYS
IN THE
HISTORY
OF THE
HAWAIIAN
NATION

1893-1993

Sanford B. Dole is inaugurated as the first appointed governor of the Territory of Hawai'i, June 15, 1900. (Hawai'i State Archives photo)

101

THE
OVERTHROW
OF THE
HAWAIIAN
KINGDOM

The Queen's plea and the opposition of the Hawaiian people were ignored by a nation which claimed to be devoted to liberty and the inalienable right of self-determination. On July 7, 1898, as the Spanish-American War reinforced the need for a strong military presence in the Pacific, President McKinley signed the Newlands Joint Resolution which annexed Hawai'i. This was the first and only annexation of any new territory in the history of the United States achieved through resolution.

The self-declared Republic of Hawai'i ceded sovereignty over the Hawaiian islands to the United States through the Newlands Joint Resolution.

This included the ceding of 1.8 million acres of crown, government and public lands of the Kingdom of Hawai'i, without the consent of, or compensation to, the Native Hawaiian people or their sovereign government. The U.S. Congress ratified the cession, annexed Hawai'i and vested title to the lands in Hawai'i with the United States.

On Annexation Day, American Blue Jackets and Marines from the *U.S.S. Philadelphia* landed in Hawai'i to take part in the ceremonies at 'Iolani Palace. The flag of Hawai'i was lowered for the last time on August 12, 1898, Annexation Day. Queen Lili'uokalani remained at Washington Place that day, surrounded by family, nobles, and other loyalists who refused to attend the "grand ceremony" of annexation and the raising of the flag of the United States.

On April 30, 1900, President McKinley signed the Organic Act that provided a government for the Territory of Hawai'i. This act defined the political infrastructure and powers of the newly established Territorial Government and its relationship to the United States. On August 21, 1959, Hawai'i became the 50th State of the United States.

The tremendous economic and social changes of 19th century Hawaii continued into the 20th as land, native language, cultural lifestyles, social prominence and political sovereignty were denied to the Hawaiian people. The consequences of this dispossession were devastating to the health and well-being of Hawaiians.

Determined to preserve their cultural identity, Hawaiians of all ages and backgrounds now looked to the centennial observances as a new beginning for self-determination and self-governance.

'ONIPA'A
FIVE DAYS
IN THE
HISTORY
OF THE
HAWAIIAN
NATION

1893-1993

CHAPTER EIGHT

January 17, 1993:
After A Century of Dishonor,
A Nation Reunited

"I could not turn back the time for the political change, but there is still time to save our heritage. You must remember never to cease to act because you fear you may fail. The way to lose any earthly kingdom is to be inflexible, intolerant, and prejudicial. Another way is to be too flexible, tolerant of too many wrongs and without judgement at all. It is a razor's edge. It is the width of a blade of pili grass. To gain the kingdom of heaven is to hear what is not said, to see what cannot be seen, and to know the unknowable -- that is Aloha. All things in this world are two; in heaven there is but One."

Lili'uokalani, 1917
(As reported by her hānai daughter, Lydia K. Aholo to Helena G. Allen, The Betrayal of Lili'uokalani, Mutual Publishing, 1982.)

*A*s sunlight warmed Nuʻuanu Valley and the gentle winds from the Pali graced Mauna ʻAla, Hawaiian royal societies led by the Royal Order of Kamehameha began their early morning ceremonies at the sacred resting place of their beloved royalty.

They gathered to honor Queen Liliʻuokalani's courage and perseverance during difficult times. They openly acknowledged the grave injustice perpetrated 100 years ago and renewed their Queen's plea to the U.S. government to allow justice to prevail. The societies prayed for the restoration of the honor of the Hawaiian people through a new reconciliation between their nation and the U.S. government.

As the royal societies prepared for the day with prayer, Pilikana O Nā Koʻolauloa, a group from windward Oʻahu, greeted the dawn on a solemn march at 4:30 a.m. at Nuʻuanu Pali. Later in the morning, they joined other Hawaiian groups that had marched from points around Oʻahu to gather on the grounds of ʻIolani Palace, which was draped in black mourning cloth.

Marching from Aloha Tower, an astoundingly large crowd of 16,000 people rallied together under the sponsorship of Ka Lāhui Hawaiʻi. With conch shells blowing and chants of *"ʻike pono,"* marchers with flags, signs and banners streamed in to fill the grounds. Persons of all ages and from every island, members of Hawaiian groups, non-Hawaiians, and visitors from around the world came together in a strong and moving show of solidarity for Hawaiian self-determination. A convoy of trucks and motorcycles slowly passed in front of the Palace on King Street, while throughout the day people on the sidewalks held home-made signs showing their commitment to Hawaiian sovereignty.

Though it seemed that the Capitol district could hold no more, still the Hawaiians kept gathering, their numbers swelling beyond estimation. The Hawaiian nation was being reunited and despite the overwhelming crowds and charged emotion, the mood of harmony always prevailed. Around the Coronation Pavilion, thousands of people listened to the *manaʻo*, the thoughts, of representatives from different Hawaiian groups. Hawaiian sovereignty was discussed from many viewpoints, all stimulating and thought-provoking. The various speakers revealed the depth and breadth of the Hawaiian community's commitment to restore a nation's sovereignty, and the discussion traveled to every small group that had gathered on the grounds. Everywhere one looked, men, women and children were talking about what had happened 100 years ago, the meaning of sovereignty or what this day meant in the life of a native people. It was not uncommon to also see tears flow which had been held back for many years.

ʻONIPAʻA
FIVE DAYS
IN THE
HISTORY
OF THE
HAWAIIAN
NATION

1893-1993

(Previous page) Thousands of Hawaiians march down Mililani Street toward ʻIolani Palace in solemn remembrance of the overthrow of the Hawaiian monarchy. (OHA photo by Deborah Ward)

The Royal Societies enter the Royal Mausoleum at Mauna ‘Ala early Sunday morning, January 17, 1993 to honor departed *ali‘i*. (Douglas Peebles photo)

107

AFTER A
CENTURY OF
DISHONOR
A NATION
REUNITED

The Royal Societies pay homage at the tomb of the Kalākaua family. (Douglas Peebles photo)

The spirit of unity that prevailed throughout the day was symbolized during an *'awa* ceremony held by the Council of Hawaiian Organizations and Ka Pākaukau on the 'Iolani Palace grounds that morning. *'Awa* drinking began when gods mingled with men. *'Awa* came from the realm of the gods who gave the plant to man. Traditionally, *'awa* was an important part of many different rituals, including the taking of solemn vows. With Sam Ka'ai as *kahu* of the ceremony, the participants in this ritual came together for the purpose

of unification and to solidify their commitment to the self-determination and sovereignty of the Hawaiian people.

In another ceremony of unification and healing, the United Church of Christ (UCC) formally apologized for "our denomination's historical complicity in the illegal overthrow of the Hawaiian Monarchy in 1893." "An Apology to the Indigenous Hawaiian People" was delivered that Sunday by the Reverend Dr. Paul Sherry, national President of the UCC, at the Coronation Pavilion and later at Kaumakapili Church in Honolulu. As the successor to the Congregational churches which were first established in Hawai'i by American Protestant missionaries in 1820, the United Church of Christ acknowledged the dual legacy of Hawai'i's American missionaries:

> *"We remember that in 1820 the American Board of Commissioners for Foreign Missions sent missionaries to Hawai'i to preach the good news of Jesus Christ. These men and women, often at great personal sacrifice, witnessed the Gospel in compelling ways. Their lives of Christian commitment and generosity are an inspiration, and their contributions endure. We thank God for them.*
>
> *Some of these men and women, however, sometimes confused the ways of the West with the ways of Christ. Assumptions of cultural and racial superiority led some of them and those who followed them to discount or undervalue the strengths of the*

'ONIPA'A
FIVE DAYS
IN THE
HISTORY
OF THE
HAWAIIAN
NATION

1893-1993

Dr. Kekuni Blaisdell and Big Island homesteader Sonny Kaniho greet each other in a traditional Hawaiian embrace, reflecting the spirit of kinship that pervades 'Onipa'a. (Elizabeth Pa Martin photo)

(Facing page) For children such as Ku'ulei and Tierra Lucht, these days will open their eyes to the past while instilling pride for the future. Here they collect signatures to support Governor Waihe'e's decision to fly Hawai'i's flag alone. (Elizabeth Pa Martin photo)

AFTER A
CENTURY OF
DISHONOR
A NATION
REUNITED

'ONIPA'A
FIVE DAYS
IN THE
HISTORY
OF THE
HAWAIIAN
NATION

1893-1993

111

AFTER A
CENTURY OF
DISHONOR
A NATION
REUNITED

mature society they encountered. The resulting social, political, and economic implications of these harmful attitudes contributed to the suffering of the Native Hawaiian people in that time and into the present."

For many Hawaiians who are devout Christians, the apology of the United Church of Christ helped reconcile their personal faith with what they had long known of their history. Although the apology stirred controversy and debate, it was another step toward bridging the divisions within the community through a cleansing of the past.

112

'ONIPA'A
FIVE DAYS
IN THE
HISTORY
OF THE
HAWAIIAN
NATION

1893-1993

On Sunday afternoon, a crowd of onlookers who had squeezed onto Mililani Street on the *'Ewa* side of Ali'iōlani Hale watched another aspect of Hawai'i's past unfold. While a small "living history" detachment of 1893 U.S. troops guarded what was once the site of Arion Hall, costumed role-players were ensconced across the street for the re-creation of the reading of a proclamation that declared the Hawaiian Kingdom ended and the Provisional Government established under President Sanford B. Dole. The clock of history was winding down for 1893, as dusk descended upon Honolulu.

Throughout the district the people moved toward 'Iolani Palace, whose stately portals were cast in a golden hue by the setting sun.

(Previous page) Hawaiians from the island of Hawai'i travel to O'ahu to join in a historic march in support of Hawaiian sovereignty. By later in the afternoon, thousands of *kānaka maoli* from all the Hawaiian islands gathered on the grounds of 'Iolani Palace. (OHA photo by Deborah Ward)

113

AFTER A
CENTURY OF
DISHONOR
A NATION
REUNITED

Kawika Liu, Kahele Dukelow and Kaleikoa Kā'eo, University of Hawai'i students, chant as they march toward 'Iolani Palace grounds. (OHA photo by Jeff Clark)

'ONIPA'A
FIVE DAYS
IN THE
HISTORY
OF THE
HAWAIIAN
NATION

1893-1993

AFTER A
CENTURY OF
DISHONOR
A NATION
REUNITED

Before the Hawaiian flag, generations share the pain of the overthrow of Queen Liliʻuokalani and 100 years of broken promises to her people. (*Advertiser* photo by Bruce Asato)

116

ʻONIPAʻA
FIVE DAYS
IN THE
HISTORY
OF THE
HAWAIIAN
NATION

1893-1993

(Previous page) *Pulu ʻelo i ka ua o ka hoʻoilo*, "drenched by winter's rain," is a Hawaiian poetic expression of the grief shared by Anuhea Reimann-Giegeri (*center*) with Maori friends Mamae Tuanewa Takewei (*left*) and Ngahuia Te Awekotuku for the overthrow of the Hawaiian monarchy. (*Advertiser* photo by Bruce Asato)

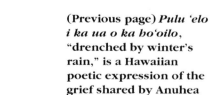

A trucker displays the Hawaiian flag from his cab as he joins in a convoy of trucks past ʻIolani Palace on King Street. As they passed the site of the 100-hour vigil, the drivers stopped to place their *hoʻokupu* on the *haka lele*. (OHA photo by Deborah Ward)

Circling ʻIolani Palace in a sign of solidarity and support for Hawaiian sovereignty, truckers blast their horns as sidewalk marchers wave the flag of Hawaiʻi. (Judiciary History Center photo)

117

AFTER A
CENTURY OF
DISHONOR
A NATION
REUNITED

Hawaiian bikers follow the truckers in a ceremonial procession around ʻIolani Palace. (Judiciary History Center photo)

118

'ONIPA'A
FIVE DAYS
IN THE
HISTORY
OF THE
HAWAIIAN
NATION

1893-1993

Kawehi Kanui of the 'Ohana Council is one of many speakers who forcefully called out this day for a restoration of the sovereign Hawaiian nation. (OHA photo by Jeff Clark)

119

AFTER A
CENTURY OF
DISHONOR
A NATION
REUNITED

One hundred years after the overthrow of the Hawaiian monarchy, a large crowd of *kānaka maoli* gather at the Coronation Pavilion to support the rebirth of their nation as various Hawaiian leaders share their thoughts in a series of stirring speeches. (Annelore Niejahr photo)

(Previous page) As "Hawai'i Pono'ī" is played, the crowd stands in respect for the national anthem of the Kingdom of Hawai'i. (OHA photo by Jeff Clark)

Gordon Pi'ianai'a and Nainoa Thompson of the Polynesian Voyaging Society join in the 'awa ceremony. (Douglas Peebles photo)

'ONIPA'A
FIVE DAYS
IN THE
HISTORY
OF THE
HAWAIIAN
NATION

1893-1993

Participating in the 'awa ceremony are (left to right) the late Kalaninuipō'aimoku Kalāhiki, H. Bruss Keppeler, Melvin Lonokaiolohia Kalāhiki, A. Frenchy Keānuenueokalaninuiamamao DeSoto, and kahu Sam Ka'ai. (Douglas Peebles photo)

123

AFTER A
CENTURY OF
DISHONOR
A NATION
REUNITED

Water from Koʻolau is poured into an *ʻawa* bowl made by Sam Kaʻai. This ancient sacred ceremony found throughout Polynesia unites the present Hawaiian generation with the traditions of their *kūpuna*. (Eileen Kalāhiki photo)

'ONIPA'A
FIVE DAYS
IN THE
HISTORY
OF THE
HAWAIIAN
NATION

1893-1993

Reverend Dr. Paul Sherry, National President of the United Church of Christ, voices a formal public apology to the Hawaiian people for the role of his church in the overthrow of the Hawaiian government and Queen Lili'uokalani. After addressing more than 20,000 people from the Coronation Pavilion on 'Iolani Palace grounds, Reverend Sherry repeated his apology later that day to the congregation at Kaumakapili Church. (OHA photo by Jeff Clark)

Reverend Paul Sherry delivers the apology to
Hawaiians on behalf of the United Church of Christ,
and a *kupuna* weeps as religious faith and national
pride are at last reconciled.
(*Advertiser* Photo by Gregory Yamamoto)

125

AFTER A
CENTURY OF
DISHONOR
A NATION
REUNITED

Reverend Kimo
Merseberg (*right*) of the
United Church of Christ
meets with Reverend
Paul Sherry and Mrs.
Sherry on 'Iolani Palace
grounds just prior to
delivery of the United
Church of Christ's
national apology. (Holly
Henderson photo)

'ONIPA'A
FIVE DAYS
IN THE
HISTORY
OF THE
HAWAIIAN
NATION

1893-1993

"U.S. troops" turn into Mililani Street near the site of Arion Hall, re-creating the illegal military invasion of Hawai'i. (Elizabeth Pa Martin photo)

Actors portrayed Japanese plantation workers who led a march to 'Iolani Palace on January 17, 1893 in support of Queen Lili'uokalani. Although the workers were urged by their Consul to turn back, the Japanese government at first refused to recognize the legitimacy of the Provisional Government, demanding restoration of the monarchy. (Elizabeth Pa Martin photo)

Henry Cooper (played by Neil Hulbert) reads the declaration of the Provisional Government at Aliʻiōlani Hale in the presence of other members of the Committee of Public Safety including *(left to right)* John Emmeluth (Kioni Dudley), F.W. McChesney (David Martin), Henry Waterhouse (David Eyre), H. P. Baldwin (Jack Keppeler), and W.O. Smith (Stephen Hancock). The January 17, 1893 proclamation was actually read on the steps of the building, near the U.S. military troops bivouacked at Arion Hall.
(Kendra Lucht photo)

127

AFTER A
CENTURY OF
DISHONOR
A NATION
REUNITED

(Following page) A scene from the re-enactment of the overthrow of the Hawaiian monarchy captures the attention of Chad Maeda, Tyson Chun, Roy Kupihea, Shane Ahnee and Jamie Andrade, Hawaiian Studies students from Pearl City High School. (*Star-Bulletin* photo by Mike Tsukamoto)

ʻONIPAʻA
FIVE DAYS
IN THE
HISTORY
OF THE
HAWAIIAN
NATION

1893-1993

AFTER A
CENTURY OF
DISHONOR
A NATION
REUNITED

'ONIPA'A
FIVE DAYS
IN THE
HISTORY
OF THE
HAWAIIAN
NATION

1893-1993

At the King Street entrance to the Palace grounds, "citizens of 1893" prepare for a last silent procession. The audience is subdued as green-shirted peacekeepers await the signal for the climactic closing of the re-enactment. (David Martin photo)

'Iolani Palace, draped in mournful black bunting, glows in the setting sun as thousands gather to witness the closing of the 'Onipa'a observances. (Elizabeth Pa Martin photo)

As darkness falls, Queen Liliʻuokalani (portrayed by Leo Anderson Akana) reads her proclamation yielding to the superior forces of the United States. The Queen then calls upon the American government to reverse the actions of its representatives, perpetuating the sovereignty of the land through righteousness. (Deborah Uchida photo)

The procession of the Queen's loyal subjects gathers at the Palace steps to hear Liliʻuokalani speak on the destiny of the Hawaiian monarchy. (OHA photo by Deborah Ward)

'ONIPA'A
FIVE DAYS
IN THE
HISTORY
OF THE
HAWAIIAN
NATION

1893-1993

Members of the Council of Hawaiian Organizations prepare for closing the 100-hour vigil at the Hale Mana Aloha Vigil site with a torchlight procession to 'Iolani Palace.
(Judiciary History Center photo)

133

AFTER A
CENTURY OF
DISHONOR
A NATION
REUNITED

(Following page)
Torchbearers pass the
statue of Kamehameha I
as they proceed to the
Palace grounds. Hawai-
ians of all ages carried
the torches in remem-
brance for the past and
hope for the future.
(*Advertiser* photo by
Gregory Yamamoto)

Twenty thousand people watch as torchbearers enter the grounds of ʻIolani
Palace. Organized by the Council of Hawaiian Organizations, the torchlight
ceremony will remain one of the most haunting memories of these five historic
days. (Previous page, bottom-Judiciary History Center photo; This page, top-
Douglas Peebles photo; bottom-Deborah Uchida photo)

'ONIPA'A
FIVE DAYS
IN THE
HISTORY
OF THE
HAWAIIAN
NATION

1893-1993

AFTER A
CENTURY OF
DISHONOR
A NATION
REUNITED

At the steps of 'Iolani Palace, thousands of Hawaiians, their friends and supporters, waited as the sun slowly set. For the last time, they were gathered to witness a historical re-enactment, the most tragic in the series of "living history" moments. From behind the glass-paneled doors of the Palace emerged Queen Lili'uokalani, portrayed with dignity by Leo Anderson Akana. Her words would move the audience to silence and tears.

"Now, to avoid any collision of armed forces, and perhaps the loss of life, I do, under this protest and impelled by said forces, yield my authority until such time as the government of the United States shall, upon the facts being presented to it, undo the action of its representative, and reinstate me in the authority which I claim as the constitutional sovereign of the Hawaiian Islands."

After reading her statement, Lili'uokalani looked out at the silent, solemn thousands and spoke to them across the span of time:

"Now, my people, hear these words of mine that I say to you in our dark hour. Hold yourselves up high and be proud. For each and everyone of you has much to be proud of in yourselves and in your people.

"Hold fast to that pride and love you have for your heritage and your country. Yes, your country. For your nation — 'Onipa'a. Hold fast!"

The Queen then walked alone into the darkness of the Palace. Its grounds were completely dark

'ONIPA'A
FIVE DAYS
IN THE
HISTORY
OF THE
HAWAIIAN
NATION

1893-1993

State Senator Eloise Ululani Tungpalan delivers her closing remarks, ending the 100-hour vigil in remembrance of the overthrow of the Hawaiian monarchy. (OHA photo by Jeff Clark)

when a single light went on in the room which had once been Liliʻuokalani's prison, as a symbol of the Hawaiian people's loss of freedom and sovereignty.

A procession of 100 torches was moving at that moment from Kawaiahaʻo Church, solemnly winding its way down King Street to the steps of ʻIolani Palace. The night blazed with the timelessness of torchlight as the Council of Hawaiian Organizations lit each torch with the flame which had burned continuously throughout the 100-hour vigil. The torchbearers were members of the Council, Kamehameha Schools students, and members of the public. "I just feel the hurt, grief and distress that the Queen felt," said torchbearer Chante Soma-Kalāhiki. "This is just me honoring the monarchy in a very small way. Maybe one day peace will come."

As the torchbearers walked onto the palace grounds, they were greeted with the chanting of John Keolamakaʻāinanakalāhuino Kamehameha-ʻekolu Lake, and the crowd's response of sorrow. The Hawaiian "*auē*" cannot be described; it is grief at the loss of someone or something that is held more precious than life.

A few final words were spoken that evening in recognition of hopes for a new Hawaiian nation. Extending the love and support of Polynesians from Samoa, Eni Faleomavaega, American Samoa's Delegate to Congress, addressed the injustices that had been perpetrated upon the people and nation of Hawaiʻi. State Senator A. Leiomālama Solomon shared her *manaʻo* that these five days in modern Hawaiian history would signal the "Dawn of a new Hawaiian Nation." Senator Solomon noted that "We are not Democrats. We are not Republicans. We are Hawaiians." Acknowledging the responsibility

of the United States government for the overthrow of the Hawaiian monarchy and its trust obligations to the Hawaiian people, she stressed that "We must be assured that those trust obligations are in fact met."

State Senator Eloise Ululani Tungpalan, Chair of the ʻOnipaʻa Centennial Committee, then delivered the remarks that closed the 100-hour vigil. She noted that the spirit of unity that had prevailed during these historic days would carry Hawaiians forth to the restoration of sovereignty for their nation. She then translated Queen Liliʻuokalani's composition, "The Queen's Prayer," as Palani Vaughan sang.

All but two torches were extinguished as the crowds silently left, returning home to reflect on the past 100 hours. The last two torches were placed at the statue of Queen Liliʻuokalani to illuminate her through the night.

During these last few days, new and challenging ideas had been presented to thousands of islanders; for many participants a new sense of purpose and dedication to Hawaiian sovereignty had been aroused. For many non-Hawaiians, the ʻOnipaʻa observances had been an important process of learning what their neighbors not only thought, but *felt* about issues which would certainly affect the future of everyone in the islands. And finally, who had not been touched by the spirit of *aloha* that was expressed in the midst of grief?

Self-determination, sovereignty and a renewed sense of Hawaiian pride had new meaning to those who left the Palace grounds that night. When they looked back, they saw the single light still glowing through the night in the Queen's chambers. Her light remained a beacon to her people as they moved together into the future.

137

AFTER A
CENTURY OF
DISHONOR
A NATION
REUNITED

138

'ONIPA'A
FIVE DAYS
IN THE
HISTORY
OF THE
HAWAIIAN
NATION

1893-1993

The splendor of Queen Lili'uokalani's statue is enhanced with the multitude of *ho'okupu* from the people of Hawai'i. (Photo Elizabeth Pa Martin)

EPILOGUE
To Restore a Nation

On the morning after the 'Onipa'a observances, floral offerings grace the steps of 'Iolani Palace. (Holly Henderson photo)

140

'ONIPA'A
FIVE DAYS
IN THE
HISTORY
OF THE
HAWAIIAN
NATION

1893-1993

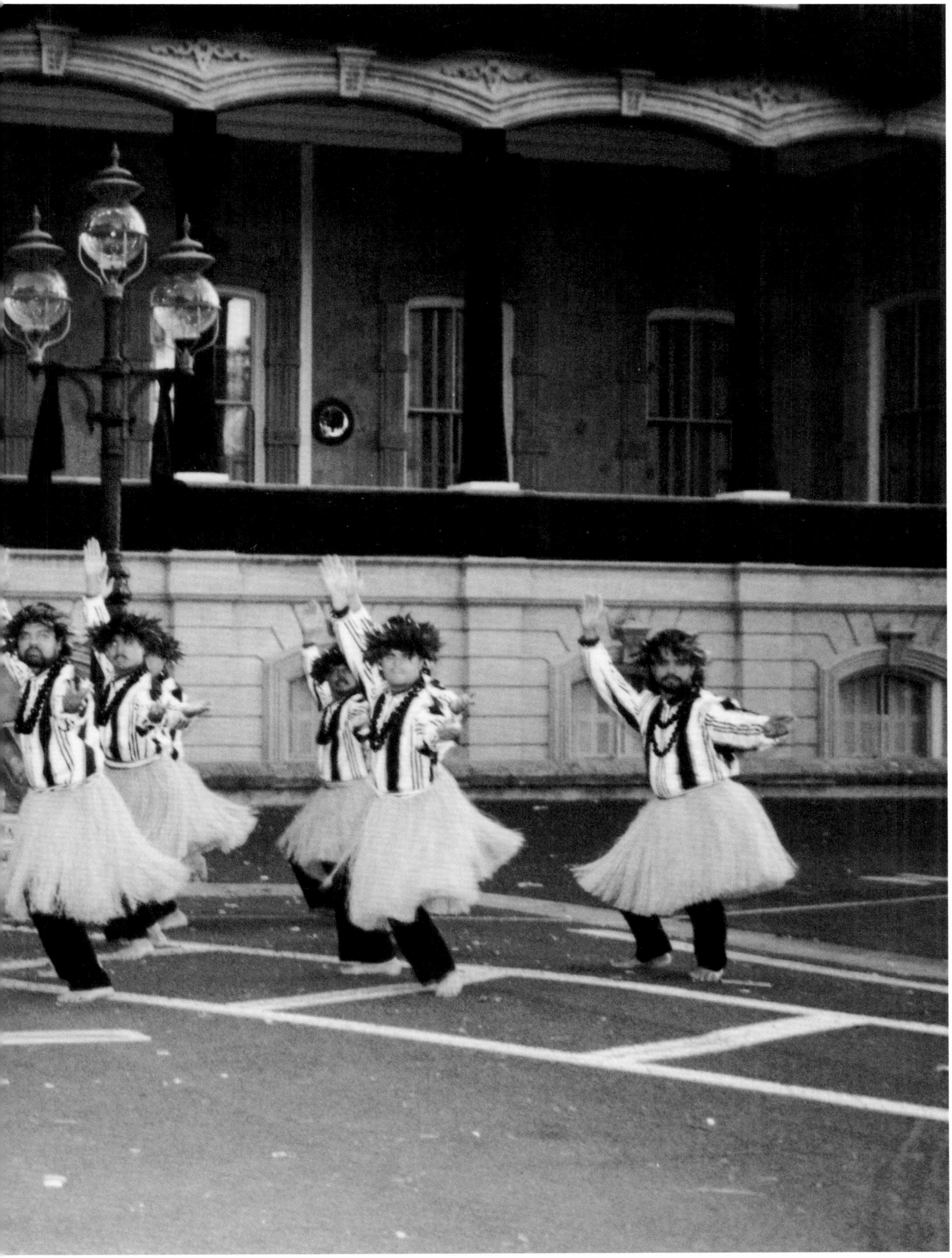

efore dawn on the morning of January 18, 1993, shadowy figures entered the gates to the 'Iolani Palace grounds. Changing from street clothes to the costumes of traditional *hula* dancers, they tied the *kūpe'e* to their wrists and ankles, the *lei 'ā'ī,* and the *lei po'o.*

These men and women were preparing for a ritual that only a few would witness. They came to bring a quiet closure, through prayer, chant, and *hula,* to the events of the prior week, to the last century. Offered as *ho'okupu* by 'Onipa'a Committee members Leinā'ala Kalama Heine and R.M. Keahi Allen, this rite was the traditional Hawaiian way to complete important events.

As the sun began to rise, Hālau Nā Kamalei led by *kumu hula* Robert Uluwehi Cazimero and Hālau Nā Pualei O Likolehua led by *kumu hula* Leinā'ala Kalama Heine offered a prayer, then moved to the front steps of 'Iolani Palace. In the soft dawn light they offered traditional dances and chants which said, in part, that it was time to move forward, allowing the past to be the foundation and guide, and to focus on the future of the Hawaiian race.

In the days following the 'Onipa'a observance, discussions concerning

142

'ONIPA'A
FIVE DAYS
IN THE
HISTORY
OF THE
HAWAIIAN
NATION

1893-1993

(Previous Page) At dawn on January 18, 1993, Hālau Nā Kamalei, under the direction of *kumu hula* Robert Uluwehi Cazimero, ushers in a new beginning for the Hawaiian nation. (Elizabeth Pa Martin photo)

***Kumu hula* Leinā'ala Kalama Heine's Hālau Nā Pualei O Likolehua chants and dances to the promise of a new future where past injustices will be properly addressed and problems resolved. (Elizabeth Pa Martin photo)**

(Facing Page) In the pre-dawn darkness, *kumu hula* Leinā'ala Kalama Heine prepares for the morning ceremony that will mark the closure of the 'Onipa'a observances. (Elizabeth Pa Martin photo)

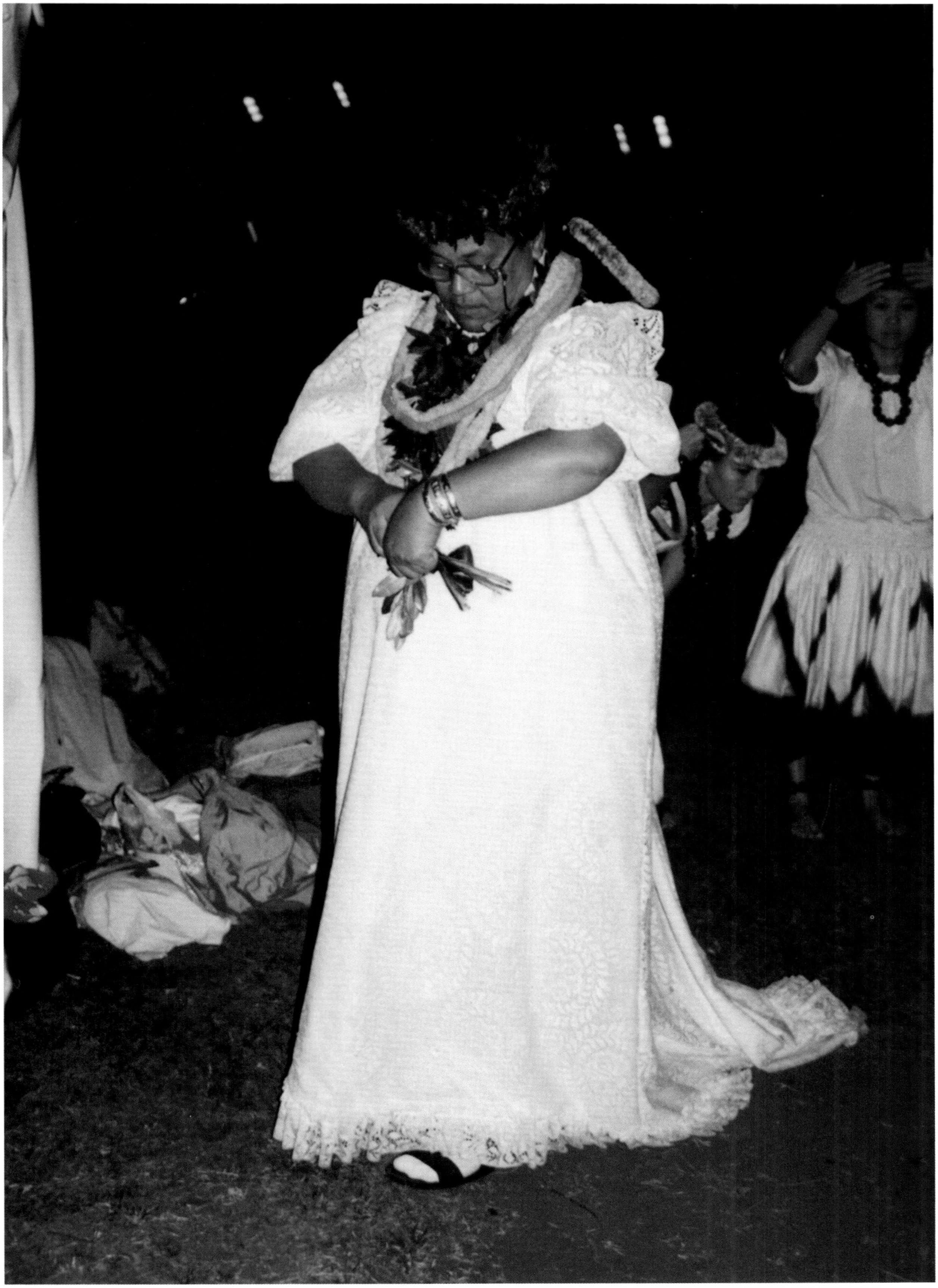

144

'ONIPA'A
FIVE DAYS
IN THE
HISTORY
OF THE
HAWAIIAN
NATION

1893-1993

"Betrayal," with Marlene Sai as Queen Lili'uokalani, was aired on the evening of January 17, 1993 on Hawai'i Public Television. The docu-drama dramatized the events surrounding the illegal overthrow of the Hawaiian monarchy. (Kukui Foundation photo)

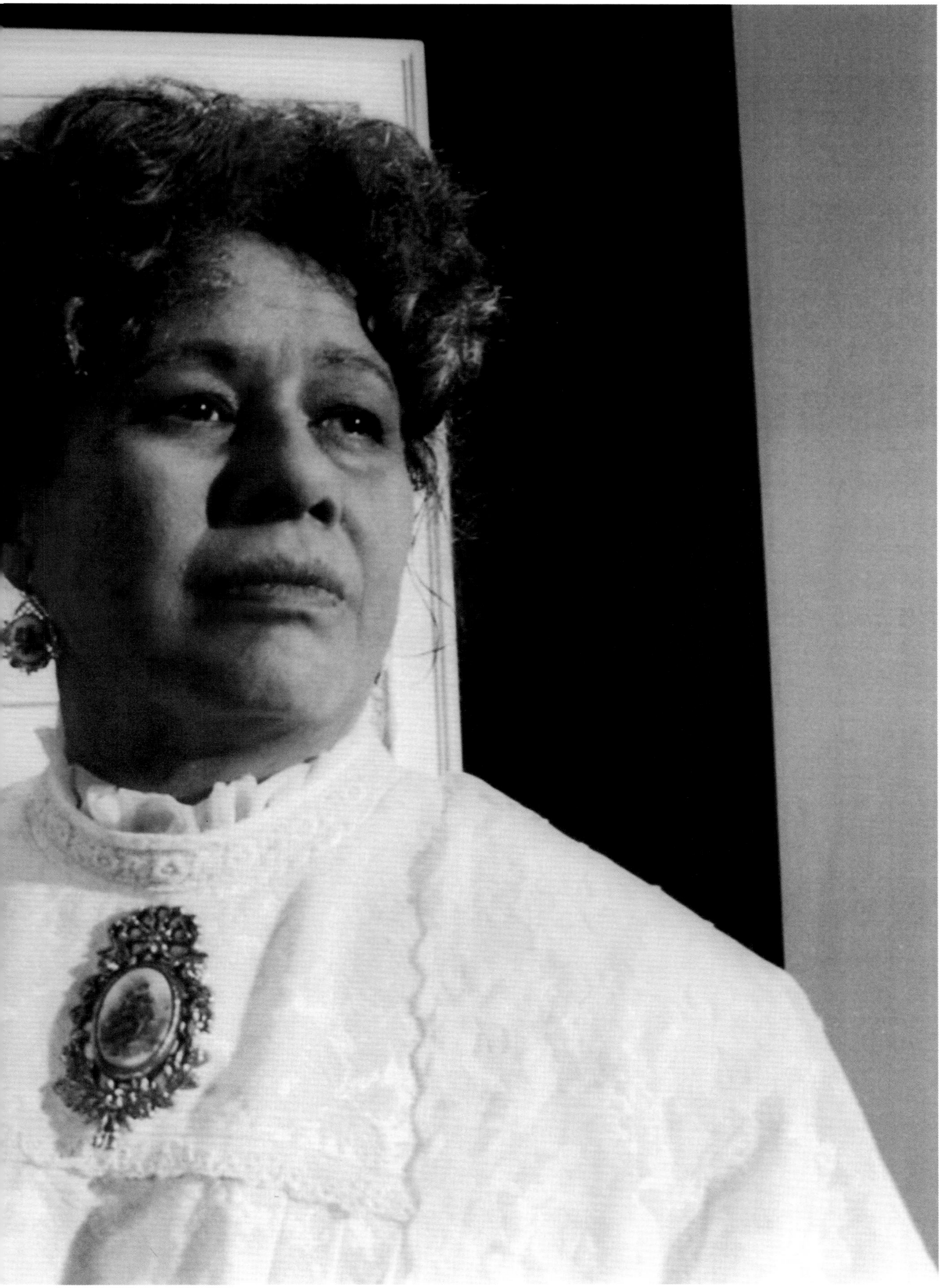

Hawaiian sovereignty were being held everywhere: in the press, in schoolrooms, in offices, in backyard gatherings, in political meetings, and over the dinner table. What once had been seen as an impossible idea promoted by only the most radical fringe was now a commitment to Hawaiian self-determination supported by *kūpuna*, teachers, community leaders and just regular folk who had become aware of their history and now wanted to act on their future. For those who had not attended the Honolulu activities, not only had all the islands organized their own sovereignty marches and events, but KHET broadcast an original drama depicting the overthrow of the Hawaiian monarchy. "Betrayal," starring Marlene Sai as Queen Liliʻuokalani, aired on public television Sunday evening, January 17, 1993.

The ʻOnipaʻa observances were not confined to Oʻahu. On January 9, 1993, on the island of Kauaʻi, a march for sovereignty was held; similar sovereignty activities took place on the island of Hawaiʻi. Plans for the Maui ʻOnipaʻa Centennial were coordinated by Maui Hawaiian Agencies and Organizations with Ed Lindsey serving as chairperson. A play portraying the overthrow was staged as one of the main events. Boy Kanaʻe took primary responsibility for presenting the play, written by Robin Kalama, Leslie Kuloloio and Margo Berdeshevsky. At midnight a vigil was also organized by the group, the Hawaiian Nation, headed by Meling Akuna.

Nationally, the "Overthrow in Five Acts" earned Hui Naʻauao an Award of Merit from the American Association for State and Local History (AASLH). An organization dedicated to the professional enhancement of local history through collection, preservation, research and interpretation, the AASLH noted that the pageant was planned and written with a high degree of thoroughness and historical accuracy.

The impetus given Hawaiian sovereignty by the ʻOnipaʻa observances carried over to the Hawaiʻi State Legislature, which opened just a few days later. Several Hawaiian organizations, including Ka Lāhui Hawaiʻi and Pilikana O Koʻolauloa, marched to the State Capitol to meet with House and Senate leaders on the opening day of the state Legislature.

During the 1993 legislative session, hearings on Hawaiian sovereignty were held at Mabel Smyth Auditorium so that a wide variety of perspectives could be offered on how best to define and then restore sovereignty to the Hawaiian nation.

As government agencies began to respond to the call for Hawaiian self-determination, Hui Naʻauao continued to hold sovereignty workshops for Hawaiians and non-Hawaiians of all ages, backgrounds and districts. Many Native Hawaiian organizations and individuals from all islands gathered after the ʻOnipaʻa observances at Hale Naʻauao to mark a "new beginning" in their united efforts to achieve self-determination.

Attention throughout the United States to the concerns of Hawaiians was made possible during the summer of 1993 when President Bill Clinton visited the islands. Large numbers of Hawaiians demonstrated on the beach at Hilton Hawaiian Village during a special appearance there by the President. During his speech on Waikīkī Beach, President Clinton acknowledged the need for justice for the Hawaiian people and promised, "You will not be forgotten!"

Later that month, delegates and advocates of the Working Group on Indigenous Populations met in Geneva, Switzerland, under the auspices of the United Nations Geneva Conference of Indigenous Peoples. Advocates from Hawaiʻi who attended the meetings included Kealiʻi Gora and Mililani Trask from Ka Lāhui Hawaiʻi, Pōkā Laenui from the Institute for the Advancement of Hawaiian Affairs, David Martin representing the Native Hawaiian Advisory Council, Elizabeth Pa Martin for Hui Naʻauao, Kīhei Soli Nīheu of Ka Pākaukau and three spiritual leaders — George Manu, Makua Hale and Alice Smith — of Nā Koa O Puʻukoholā.

A highly discussed activity which took place in August 1993 was the People's International Tribunal which tried the United States of America on charges of crimes against *nā kānaka maoli*. Dr. Kekuni Blaisdell of Ka Pākaukau was the primary force behind the Tribunal which included re-enactments from the trial of Queen Liliʻuokalani in 1895. An outstanding physician and respected Hawaiian

ʻONIPAʻA
FIVE DAYS
IN THE
HISTORY
OF THE
HAWAIIAN
NATION

1893-1993

Kaua'i's "March for Sovereignty" ended with chanting, *hula*, and prayers at the Hikina A Ka Lā *heiau*. (Elizabeth Pa Martin photo)

TO RESTORE
A NATION

The late Helena Maka Santos, wearing a rare hibiscus *lei*, entertains Kaua'i marchers on her *'ukulele,* while Keali'i Skippy Ioane accompanies on his guitar. Many joined in the march with Hawaiian music and several moving speeches in support of Hawaiian sovereignty and self-determination. (Elizabeth Pa Martin photo)

ʻONIPAʻA
FIVE DAYS
IN THE
HISTORY
OF THE
HAWAIIAN
NATION

1893-1993

Lehua Pali (*left*), a taro farmer from Honokōhau Valley, joins Michael White, general manager of Kāʻanapali Beach Hotel, Boy Kanaʻe, a Paukukalo homesteader, and Aimoku Pali, a taro farmer from Honokōhau Valley, at the Maui ʻOnipaʻa observances. Boy Kanaʻe produced a play about the overthrow of the Hawaiian monarchy which was performed as one of the centennial activities. (Holly Henderson photo)

Michael White, Holly Henderson and Abraham Aiona, Office of Hawaiian Affairs Trustee from Maui, were also present for the Maui ʻOnipaʻa activities. (Steve Brinkman photo)

community leader, Dr. Blaisdell has for many years struggled to reverse the effects of detrimental political, health, social and cultural factors upon *nā kānaka maoli*.

The State of Hawai'i's Hawaiian Sovereignty Advisory Commission met for the first time on Saturday, August 7, 1993. Eighteen of the 19 members of the Commission were appointed by the Governor from lists submitted by Hawaiian organizations. The appointees from O'ahu are Louis K. Agard, Jr., Pōkā Laenui, Allen Hoe, Māhealani Kamau'u, Dennis "Bumpy" Kanahele, Davianna McGregor, T. 'Aimoku McClellan, William K. Meheula III, and A'o Pōhaku Rodenhurst. The Big Island representatives are Robert Lindsey and Ann K. Nathaniel. LaFrance Kapaka-Arboleda represents Kaua'i, Natalie "Tasha" Kama represents Maui, and Solomon Kaho'ohalahala, Jr. represents Lāna'i. Moloka'i's representative is Barbara Hanchett Kalipi. The representative from Ni'ihau is Ilei Beniamina. The ex-officio representative from America was the late Victor A. Jarrett of Las Vegas. Kīna'u Boyd Kamali'i represents the Office of Hawaiian Affairs, Kamaki K. Kanahele III the State Council of Hawaiian Homestead Associations, and H. K. Bruss Keppeler the Association of Hawaiian Civic Clubs.

Choosing the best path to achieve Hawaiian sovereignty remains the great task, born in the faith that justice must prevail. From the Office of Hawaiian Affairs, from the Hawaiian Sovereignty Advisory Commission, from the many Hawaiian sovereignty groups, Hawaiian organizations and clubs to individual Hawaiians of all ages and backgrounds, the unity of purpose manifested during the centennial observances of the overthrow of the Hawaiian monarchy will prevail.

During these observances, nature seemed to respond to the activities taking place on the Palace grounds. Once when "Hawai'i Pono'ī" was being played, a sharp wind suddenly unfurled the Royal Standard above 'Iolani Palace and a rainbow appeared. When the re-creation of the landing of the U.S. troops took place, a dark drizzle suddenly fell upon the proceedings. During a chant remembering the ancestral spirits before the burial mound on the Palace grounds, the sky darkened and again a light rain fell, stopping only when the chanting was finished.

Within the *na'au* of the Hawaiian people is the powerful legacy of an ancient civilization that could achieve the impossible. The Hawaiian people will draw upon that heritage to build a nation for the betterment and enrichment of all lives within the Hawaiian islands. **ʻONIPAʻA**

(Following page) Young men from the island of Hawai'i offer floral *ho'okupu* in the memory of Queen Lili'uokalani as they join other *hālau hula* performing in the 'Onipa'a ceremony in Hilo's Edith Kanaka'ole Tennis Stadium. (*Star-Bulletin* photo by Rod Thompson)

150

'ONIPA'A
FIVE DAYS
IN THE
HISTORY
OF THE
HAWAIIAN
NATION

1893-1993

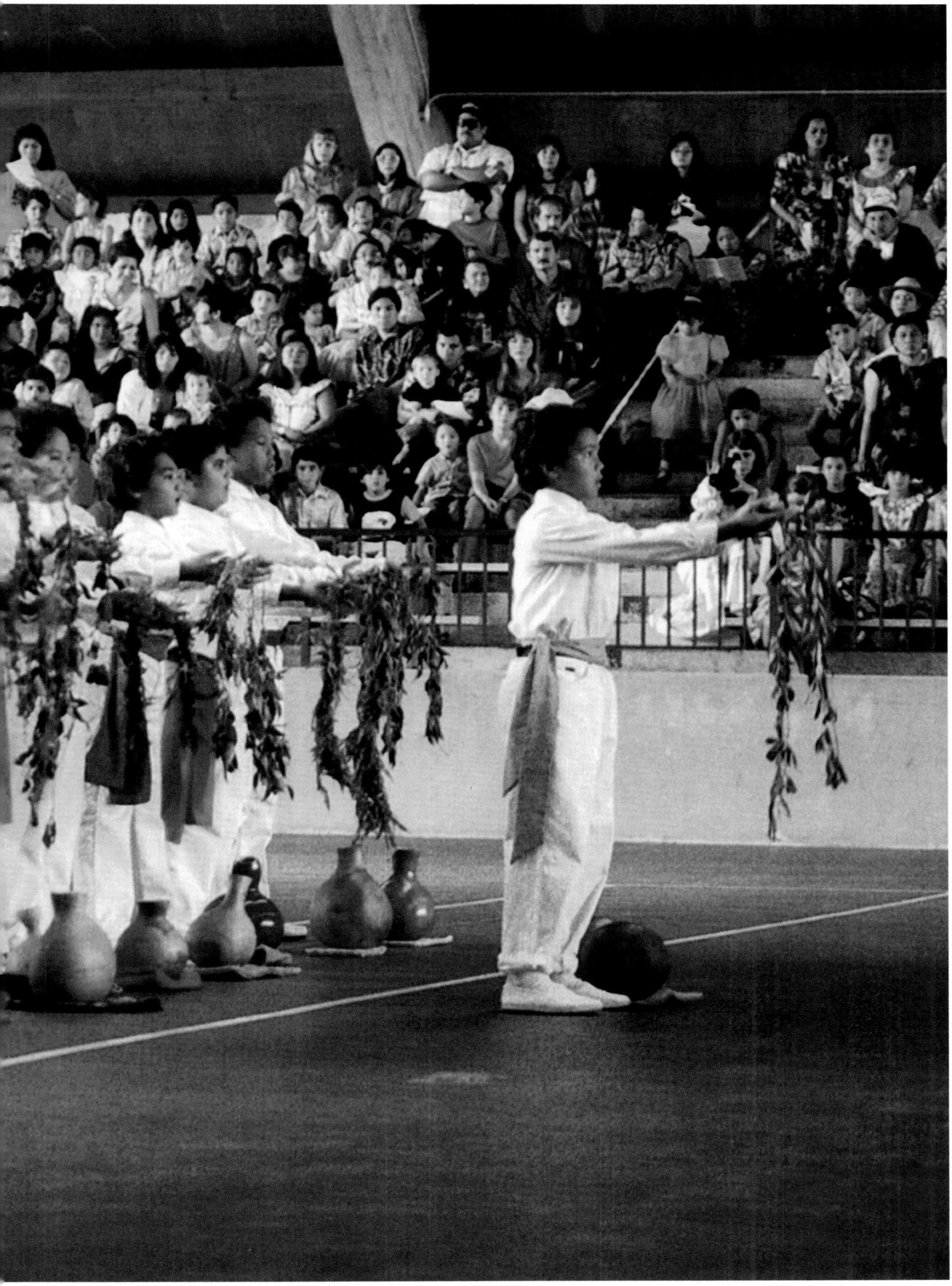

'ONIPA'A
FIVE DAYS
IN THE
HISTORY
OF THE
HAWAIIAN
NATION

1893-1993

January 18, 1993—The morning after, Liko and Ho'oulu Hee clean up the little debris left as an exhausted but happy Keahi Allen looks on. Life goes on. (Holly Henderson photo)

"You will not be forgotten," President Bill Clinton promises the Hawaiian people on July 11, 1993 during a public address on Waikīkī Beach. The Congress of the United States and President Clinton partially fulfilled that pledge on November 23, 1993 when they apologized for the illegal overthrow of the Hawaiian Kingdom and supported reconciliation efforts between the United States and the Native Hawaiian people. (*Advertiser* photo by Carl Viti)

100TH ANNIVERSARY OF THE OVERTHROW
OF THE HAWAIIAN KINGDOM

Public Law 103-150,103rd Congress, Joint Resolution

To acknowledge the 100th anniversary of the January 17, 1893 overthrow of the Kingdom of Hawaii, and to offer an apology to Native Hawaiians on behalf of the United States for the overthrow of the Kingdom of Hawaii.

Whereas, prior to the arrival of the first Europeans in 1778, the Native Hawaiian people lived in a highly organized, self-sufficient, subsistent social system based on communal land tenure with a sophisticated language, culture, and religion;

Whereas a unified monarchical government of the Hawaiian Islands was established in 1810 under Kamehameha I, the first King of Hawaii;

Whereas, from 1826 until 1893, the United States recognized the independence of the Kingdom of Hawaii, extended full and complete diplomatic recognition to the Hawaiian Government, and entered into treaties and conventions with the Hawaiian monarchs to govern commerce and navigation in 1826, 1842, 1849, 1875, and 1887;

Whereas the Congregational Church (now known as the United Church of Christ), through its American Board of Commissioners for Foreign Missions, sponsored and sent more than 100 missionaries to the Kingdom of Hawaii between 1820 and 1850;

Whereas, on January 14, 1893, John L. Stevens (hereafter referred to in this Resolution as the "United States Minister"), the United States Minister assigned to the sovereign and independent Kingdom of Hawaii conspired with a small group of non-Hawaiian residents of the Kingdom of Hawaii, including citizens of the United States, to overthrow the indigenous and lawful Government of Hawaii;

Whereas, in pursuance of the conspiracy to overthrow the Government of Hawaii, the United States Minister and the naval representatives of the United States caused armed naval forces of the United States to invade the sovereign Hawaiian nation on January 16, 1893, and to position themselves near the Hawaiian Government buildings and the Iolani Palace to intimidate Queen Liliuokalani and her Government;

Whereas, on the afternoon of January 17, 1893, a Committee of Safety that represented the American and European sugar planters, descendents of missionaries, and financiers deposed the Hawaiian monarchy and proclaimed the establishment of a Provisional Government;

Whereas the United States Minister thereupon extended diplomatic recognition to the Provisional Government that was formed by the conspirators without the consent of the Native Hawaiian people or the lawful Government of Hawaii and in violation of treaties between the two nations and of international law

Whereas, soon thereafter, when informed of the risk of bloodshed with resistance, Queen Liliuokalani issued the following statement yielding her authority to the United States Government rather than to the Provisional Government:

"I Liliuokalani, by the Grace of God and under the Constitution of the Hawaiian Kingdom, Queen, do hereby solemnly protest against any and all acts done against myself and the Constitutional Government of the Hawaiian Kingdom by certain persons claiming to have established a Provisional Government of and for this Kingdom."

"That I yield to the superior force of the United States of America whose Minister Plenipotentiary, His Excellency John L. Stevens, has caused United States troops to be landed at Honolulu and declared that he would support the Provisional Government.

"Now to avoid any collision of armed forces, and perhaps the loss of life, I do this under protest and impelled by said force yield my authority until such time as the Government of the United States shall, upon facts being presented to it, undo the action of its representatives and reinstate me in the authority which I claim as the Constitutional Sovereign of the Hawaiian Islands."
Done at Honolulu this 17th day of January, A.D. 1893.;

Whereas, without the active support and intervention by the United States diplomatic and military representatives, the insurrection against the Government of Queen Liliuokalani would have failed for lack of popular support and insufficient arms;

Whereas, on February 1, 1893, the United States Minister raised the American flag and proclaimed Hawaii to be a protectorate of the United States;

Whereas the report of a Presidentially established investigation conducted by former Congressman James Blount into the events surrounding the insurrection and overthrow of January 17, 1893 concluded that the United States diplomatic and military representatives had abused their authority and were responsible for the change in government;

Whereas, as a result of this investigation, the United States Minister to Hawaii was recalled from his diplomatic post and the military commander of the United States armed forces stationed in Hawaii was disciplined and forced to resign his commission;

Whereas, in a message to Congress on December 18, 1893, President Grover Cleveland reported fully and accurately on the illegal acts of the conspirators, described such acts as an "act of war, committed with the participation of a diplomatic representative of the United States and without authority of Congress", and acknowledged that by such acts the government of a peaceful and friendly people was overthrown;

Whereas President Cleveland further concluded that a "substantial wrong has thus been done which a due regard for our national character as well as the rights of the injured people requires we should endeavor to repair" and called for the restoration of the Hawaiian monarchy;

Whereas the Provisional Government protested President Cleveland's call for the restoration of the monarchy and continued to hold state power and pursue annexation to the United States;

Whereas the Provisional Government successfully lobbied the Committee on Foreign Relations of the Senate (hereafter referred to in this Resolution as the "Committee") to conduct a new investigation into the events surrounding the overthrow of the monarchy;

Whereas the Committee and its chairman, Senator John Morgan conducted hearings in Washington, D.C., from December 27, 1893 through February 26, 1894, in which members of the Provisional Government justified and condoned the actions of the United States Minister and recommended annexation of Hawaii;

Whereas, although the Provisional Government was able

154

'ONIPA'A
FIVE DAYS
IN THE
HISTORY
OF THE
HAWAIIAN
NATION

1893-1993

to obscure the role of the United States in the illegal over-throw of the Hawaiian monarchy, it was unable to rally the support from two-thirds of the Senate needed to ratify a treaty of annexation;

Whereas, on July 4, 1894, the Provisional Government declared itself to be the Republic of Hawaii;

Whereas, on January 24, 1895, while imprisoned in Iolani Palace, Queen Liliuokalani was forced by representatives of the Republic of Hawaii to officially abdicate her throne;

Whereas, in the 1896 United States Presidential election, William McKinley replaced Grover Cleveland;

Whereas, on July 7, 1898, as a consequence of the Spanish-American War, President McKinley signed the Newlands Joint Resolution that provided for the annexation of Hawaii;

Whereas, through the Newlands Resolution, the self-declared Republic of Hawaii ceded sovereignty over the Hawaiian Islands to the United States;

Whereas the Republic of Hawaii also ceded 1,800,000 acres of crown, government and public lands of the Kingdom of Hawaii, without the consent of or compensation to the Native Hawaiian people of Hawaii or their sovereign government;

Whereas the Congress, through the Newlands Resolution, ratified the cession, annexed Hawaii as part of the United States, and vested title to the lands in Hawaii in the United States;

Whereas the Newlands Resolution also specified that treaties existing between Hawaii and foreign nations were to immediately cease and be replaced by United States treaties with such nations;

Whereas the Newlands Resolution effected the transaction between the Republic of Hawaii and the United States Government;

Whereas the indigenous Hawaiian people never directly relinquished their claims to their inherent sovereignty as a people or over their national lands to the United States, either through their monarchy or through a plebiscite or referendum;

Whereas, on April 30, 1900, President McKinley signed the Organic Act that provided a government for the territory of Hawaii and defined the political structure and powers of the newly established Territorial Government and its relation-ship to the United States;

Whereas, on August 21, 1959, Hawaii became the 50th State of the United States;

Whereas the health and well-being of the Native Hawaiian people is intrinsically tied to their deep feelings and attachment to the land;

Whereas the long-range economic and social changes in Hawaii over the nineteenth and early twentieth centuries have been devastating to the population and to the health and well-being of the Hawaiian people;

Whereas the Native Hawaiian people are determined to preserve, develop and transmit to future generations their ancestral territory, and their cultural identity in accordance with their own spiritual and traditional beliefs, customs, practices, language, and social institutions;

Whereas, in order to promote racial harmony and cultural understanding, the Legislature of the State of Hawaii has determined that the year 1993 should serve Hawaii as a year of special reflection on the rights and dignities of the Native Hawaiians in the Hawaiian and the American societies;

Whereas the Eighteenth General Synod of the United Church of Christ in recognition of the denomination's historical complicity in the illegal overthrow of the Kingdom of Hawaii in 1893 directed the Office of the President of the United Church of Christ to offer a public apology to the Native Hawaiian people and to initiate the process of reconciliation between the United Church of Christ and the Native Hawaiians; and

Whereas it is proper and timely for the Congress on the occasion of the impending one hundredth anniversary of the event, to acknowledge the historic significance of the illegal overthrow of the Kingdom of Hawaii, to express its deep regret to the Native Hawaiian people, and to support the reconciliation efforts of the State of Hawaii and the United Church of Christ with Native Hawaiians: Now, therefore, be it Resolved by the Senate and House of Representatives of the United States of America in Congress assembled,

SECTION 1. ACKNOWLEDGMENT AND APOLOGY.

The Congress—

(1) on the occasion of the 100th anniversary of the illegal overthrow of the Kingdom of Hawaii on January 17, 1893, acknowledges the historical significance of this event which resulted in the suppression of the inherent sovereignty of the Native Hawaiian people;

(2) recognizes and commends efforts of reconciliation initiated by the State of Hawaii and the United Church of Christ with Native Hawaiians;

(3) apologizes to Native Hawaiians on behalf of the people of the United States for the overthrow of the Kingdom of Hawaii on January 17, 1893 with the participation of agents and citizens of the United States, and the deprivation of the rights of Native Hawaiians to self-determination;

(4) expresses its commitment to acknowledge the ramifications of the overthrow of the Kingdom of Hawaii, in order to provide a proper foundation for reconciliation between the United States and the Native Hawaiian people; and

(5) urges the President of the United States to also acknowledge the ramifications of the overthrow of the Kingdom of Hawaii and to support reconciliation efforts between the United States and the Native Hawaiian people.

SEC. 2. DEFINITIONS.

As used in this Joint Resolution, the term "Native Hawaiian" means any individual who is a descendent of the aboriginal people who, prior to 1778, occupied and exercised sovereignty in the area that now constitutes the State of Hawaii.

SEC. 3. DISCLAIMER

Nothing in this Joint Resolution is intended to serve as a settlement of any claims against the United States.
Approved November 23, 1993.

LEGISLATIVE HISTORY—S.J. Res. 19:

SENATE REPORTS: No. 103-126 (Select Comm. on Indian Affairs).
CONGRESSIONAL RECORD, Vol. 139 (1993):
     Oct. 27, considered and passed Senate.
     Nov. 15, considered and passed House.
     Nov. 23, signed by President Clinton.

156

'ONIPA'A
FIVE DAYS
IN THE
HISTORY
OF THE
HAWAIIAN
NATION

1893-1993

President Clinton, shown here with (*from left to right*) Vice President Al Gore, U.S. Senator Daniel Inouye, U.S. Congresswoman Patsy Mink, U.S. Congressman Neil Abercrombie, and U.S. Senator Daniel Akaka, signs the document containing Public Law 103-150 of the 103rd Congress.

Five Days in the History of a Nation: A Color Portrait of 'Onipa'a

January 13, 1993

Nālani Olds sings "Ku'u Pua I Paoakalani," one of Queen Lili'uokalani's own compositions, at the opening ceremonies. Nālani's great-grandmother, Ellen Wright Prendergast, lady-in-waiting to the Queen, was the composer of the anti-annexation song "Kaulana Nā Pua." (Deborah Uchida photo)

158

'ONIPA'A
FIVE DAYS
IN THE
HISTORY
OF THE
HAWAIIAN
NATION

1893-1993

The Hawaiian flag flies at half-staff at Union Station in Washington, D.C., while thousands of miles away, the 'Onipa'a observances commence. Through the successful efforts of Hawai'i's U.S. Senator Daniel Akaka, Hawai'i's standard will remain at this traditional position of mourning during the next four days. (Joseph Chang photo)

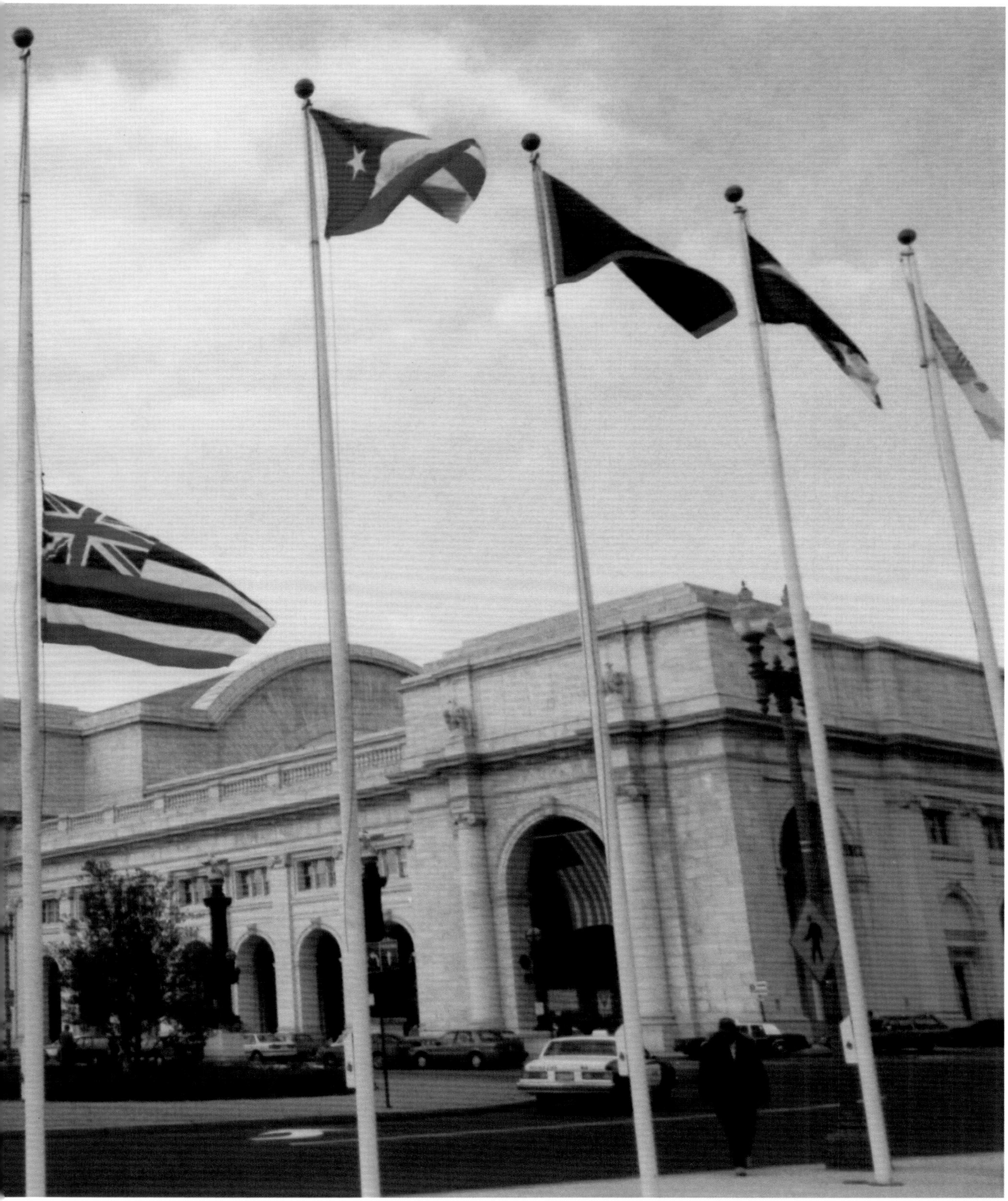

The audience at the 'Onipa'a opening ceremony shade themselves with commemorative booklets as the five-day observance formally begins with traditional prayers, floral offerings, music and messages from a variety of dignitaries. (Deborah Uchida photo)

'ONIPA'A
FIVE DAYS
IN THE
HISTORY
OF THE
HAWAIIAN
NATION

1893-1993

Hawai'i's political and spiritual leaders gather at the opening ceremony to honor the memory of Queen Lili'uokalani and to acknowledge the Hawaiian right to sovereignty. Governor John Waihe'e is seated with (*left to right*) U.S. Congresswoman Patsy Mink, 'Onipa'a Chair State Senator Eloise Ululani Tungpalan, Office of Hawaiian Affairs Chairman Clayton Hee and Reverend William Kaina of Kawaiaha'o Church. Renowned Hawaiian chanter John Keolamaka'āinanakalāhuino Kamehameha-'ekolu Lake stands behind the dignitaries as he prepares to deliver a chant in honor of his ancestor, ancient Chief Iwikauikaua. (Deborah Uchida photo)

Renwick Joe Tassill and the late Randy Heano Kalāhiki of the Council of Hawaiian Organizations hold two of the four torches which were lit at the beginning of the ceremony at noon. *Pū* trumpeter Richard "Babe" Bell waits for his cue. (OHA photo by Deborah Ward)

'Onipa'a Chair, State Senator Eloise Ululani Tungpalan delivers welcoming remarks to the hundreds of dignitaries, community leaders and general public who attended the opening ceremonies. President of the Council of Hawaiian Organizations Melvin Kalāhiki, also an 'Onipa'a Centennial Observance Committee member, stands to the right of the Senator. (OHA photo by Deborah Ward)

162

'ONIPA'A
FIVE DAYS
IN THE
HISTORY
OF THE
HAWAIIAN
NATION

1893-1993

(Facing page) Ednel Hahue, who is pure Hawaiian, proudly carried the Hawaiian flag at the opening ceremonies. (*Advertiser* photo by Carl Viti)

William Lau of the Royal Order of Kamehameha places *hoʻokupu* at the Queen's statue. (Deborah Uchida photo)

The *kūpuna* of Ka Lāhui Hawai'i commence their three-night vigil at 'Iolani Palace to ask forgiveness for all wrongs done to and by the Hawaiian people. (*Star-Bulletin* photo by Ken Ige)

'ONIPA'A
FIVE DAYS
IN THE
HISTORY
OF THE
HAWAIIAN
NATION

1893-1993

Sam Ka'ai (*right foreground*) intones a traditional chant in front of Ali'iōlani Hale to begin the 100-hour vigil. (*Advertiser* photo by Gregory Yamamoto)

A replica of Queen Lili'uokalani's royal standard is displayed above the *ho'okupu* table inside the 100-hour vigil tent of the Council of Hawaiian Organizations. Beautifully reproduced from the original design by Kalaninuipō'aimoku Kalāhiki, David "Bully" Kaina and Melvin Kalāhiki, this flag was carried in the first "Queen Lili'uokalani Aloha Peace Walk" held on September 2, 1992. (Elizabeth Pa Martin photo)

Torchbearers stand proudly during the opening ceremony of the 100-hour vigil in front of 'Iolani Palace. (OHA photo by Deborah Ward)

166

'ONIPA'A
FIVE DAYS
IN THE
HISTORY
OF THE
HAWAIIAN
NATION

1893-1993

These torchbearers wear traditional Hawaiian garb as they join in the solemn evening procession to mark the beginning of the *kūpuna* vigil. (Douglas Peebles photo)

With torches flickering above their heads, the young women from Sacred Hearts Academy offer a musical medley in loving honor of Queen Lili'uokalani. (Douglas Peebles photo)

Opening day ceremonies conclude in the evening in front of 'Iolani Palace, where the Council of Hawaiian Organizations holds a beautiful 100-torch procession. Originally planned to represent the 100-hour vigil, the number of torches grew as more and more people spontaneously joined the procession, some bringing their own torches. (Douglas Peebles photo)

The black-draped porticos of 'Iolani Palace are illuminated by the light of the Hawaiian people's flaming torches in remembrance of past injustices. (Douglas Peebles photo)

January 14, 1993
A SPIRITUAL HOʻOKUPU AT ʻIOLANI PALACE

The honored guests at ʻIolani Palace were first escorted to the Blue Room. In this room on January 14, 1893, the Queen's ministers betrayed her by refusing to sign the new constitution. (Friends of ʻIolani Palace photo)

ʻONIPAʻA
FIVE DAYS
IN THE
HISTORY
OF THE
HAWAIIAN
NATION

1893-1993

The Throne Room of ʻIolani Palace holds a special reverence for Hawaiians who sense within this elegant chamber the ancient heritage of their *aliʻi*. During the spiritual *hoʻokupu* ceremonies, each guest was escorted into this royal sanctuary. (Friends of ʻIolani Palace photo)

Halealoha Ayau, Ipō Nihipali and Kūnani Nihipali, representing Hui Mālama i nā Kūpuna O Hawai'i nei, descend the Palace stairs in silent reflection after presenting a chant, their *ho'okupu,* in the Palace. (Elizabeth Pa Martin photo)

The Royal Hawaiian Band under the direction of Aaron Mahi, together with Yvonne Perry, performs a concert in front of 'Iolani Palace as hundreds of guests present their spiritual *ho'okupu* in the Palace and at the Queen's statue. (Elizabeth Pa Martin photo)

170

'ONIPA'A
FIVE DAYS
IN THE
HISTORY
OF THE
HAWAIIAN
NATION

1893-1993

Queen Lili'uokalani's statue overflows with floral *ho'okupu* which were reverently placed there by those who love and cherish the Queen's memory and legacy. (Elizabeth Pa Martin photo)

The spiritual *ho'okupu* of Sabra Kauka McCracken and Kaiopua Fyfe are presented at the statue of Queen Lili'uokalani.
(Elizabeth Pa Martin photo)

ALI'IŌLANI PROGRAM

Royal Guardsmen enter the Ali'iōlani Building bearing the state flag of Hawai'i and the royal standard of Queen Lili'uokalani. (David Martin photo)

H. Bruss Keppeler recounts the historical events of the Hawaiian Kingdom's last legislative session in the crowded rotunda of Ali'iōlani Hale. Queen Lili'uokalani prorogued the Legislature which met in this historic building on January 14, 1893.
(*Advertiser* photo by T. Umeda)

A COLOR PORTRAIT OF 'ONIPA'A

"We make a rainbow," are the words being sung by the Kamehameha Schools Children's Choir during the Ali'iōlani Hale ceremonies.
(*Advertiser* photo by T. Umeda)

172

'ONIPA'A
FIVE DAYS
IN THE
HISTORY
OF THE
HAWAIIAN
NATION

1893-1993

Kupuna Elizabeth Nālani Ellis welcomes the crowd to the sunrise ceremonies commencing the three-day re-enactment of the overthrow of the Hawaiian Monarchy. (Elizabeth Pa Martin photo)

Hawaiian Kingdom Legislator Joseph Nāwahi, (played by Louis Hao) shares his *mana'o* on the importance of Hawaiian independence with some of the Queen's loyal subjects, played by (*left to right*) Ki'ilei Balaz, Joseph Serrao, Nicklaus Schweizer, and Alani Apio. (Elizabeth Pa Martin photo)

Queen Lili'uokalani, played by Leo Anderson Akana, is driven by horse-drawn carriage from Ali'iōlani Hale to 'Iolani Palace in a procession that re-creates a similar event 100 years earlier. (*Advertiser* **photo by T. Umeda**)

174

'ONIPA'A
FIVE DAYS
IN THE
HISTORY
OF THE
HAWAIIAN
NATION

1893-1993

Students from Roosevelt High School prepare to enter 'Iolani Palace grounds with their chant of greeting. The students, who had spent many weeks preparing for this event, walked solemnly from their campus in Makiki to downtown Honolulu in honor of Queen Lili'uokalani and in support of Hawaiian sovereignty. (Elizabeth Pa Martin photo)

Royal Guard stand sentry at the entrance to 'Iolani Palace throughout each day of the 'Onipa'a observances. (Annelore Niejahr photo)

David Kakalia passes on the heritage of Hawaiian crafts by demonstrating one of the early steps of quiltmaking - basting on the appliqué. (Elizabeth Pa Martin photo)

KA LĀHUI NĀ KOA

UNITED STATES POST OFFICE CUSTOM HOUSE AND COURT

Nā Koa of Ka Lāhui Hawai'i stand resolutely during their vigil in front of the Old Federal Building in downtown Honolulu. A century earlier, this was the site of Arion Hall where 164 American troops stood watch over 'Iolani Palace.
(*Advertiser* photo by Gregory Yamamoto)

KŪPUNA VIGIL

Maile Akimseu, Pele Hanoa, Beth Ehu, and Clara Kakalia (*left to right*) participate in Ka Lāhui Hawai'i's *kūpuna* vigil. (Annelore Niejahr photo)

'ONIPA'A
FIVE DAYS
IN THE
HISTORY
OF THE
HAWAIIAN
NATION

1893-1993

Ho'okupu adorn the *ahu* upon its completion. (Holly Henderson photo)

January 17, 1993
ROYAL SOCIETIES AT MAUNA 'ALA

Royal Order of Kamehameha enters Mauna 'Ala, the
Royal Mausoleum in Nu'uanu Valley.
(Douglas Peebles photo)

The Royal Societies pay homage at the tomb of the
Kalākaua Dynasty. (Douglas Peebles photo)

178

'ONIPA'A
FIVE DAYS
IN THE
HISTORY
OF THE
HAWAIIAN
NATION

1893-1993

The 'Ahahui Ka'ahumanu in their traditional black *holokū* and feather *lei 'ilima* gather at Mauna 'Ala.
(Douglas Peebles photo)

THE HAWAIIAN NATION MARCHES

The streets of Honolulu are blockaded as thousands of marchers and onlookers join Kia 'Āina Mililani Trask and the officers and members of Ka Lāhui Hawai'i as they approach 'Iolani Palace. (*Advertiser* photo by Bruce Asato)

As *kumu hula* Robert Uluwehi Cazimero embraces Haunani Kay Trask of Ka Lāhui Hawai'i, *nā kumu hula* (*left to right*) Leinā'ala Kalama Heine, John Kaha'i Topolinski, Ku'ulei Punua and Māpuana de Silva join marchers gathered on the Palace grounds. These distinguished keepers of the ancient civilization had performed chants in the early morning. (*Star-Bulletin* photo by Dennis Oda)

Office of Hawaiian Affairs Trustee Samuel Kealoha (*left with child*) leads the Moloka'i delegation of Ka Lāhui Hawai'i as they join other island delegations for a reuniting of the Hawaiian nation. (Eileen Kalāhiki photo)

(Following page) Moses Kaho'okele Crabbe joins thousands of other supporters of Hawaiian sovereignty by proudly waving the flag of Hawai'i that had been designed by Kamehameha I as a symbol of his islands' independence. (*Star-Bulletin* photo by Dennis Oda)

'AWA CEREMONY

Sam Ka'ai prepares raw *'awa* during this ancient Hawaiian sacred ceremony of kinship and renewal. The *'awa* will then be poured into coconut bowls for drinking by all seated guests. (Douglas Peebles photo)

Sam Ka'ai welcomes everyone to this high *kapu*, formal *'awa* ceremony. (Douglas Peebles photo)

A COLOR PORTRAIT OF 'ONIPA'A

The Royal Order of Kamehameha, led by Ali'i 'Aimoku Edward Ka'ōpūiki, await their participation in the *'awa* ceremony. (Douglas Peebles photo)

Kayle Nākānelua of Maui holds high the first *'awa* bowl served. (Douglas Peebles photo)

Henry Cooper (played by Neil Hulbert) reads the declaration of the Provisional Government at the Mililani Street entrance of Aliʻiōlani Hale in the presence of other members of the Committee of Public Safety including (*left to right*) John Emmeluth (Kioni Dudley), F.W. McChesney (David Martin), Henry Waterhouse (David Eyre), H. P. Baldwin (Jack Keppeler), and W.O. Smith (Stephen Hancock). The January 17, 1893 proclamation was actually read on the Queen Street side of the building, behind the U.S. military troops bivouacked at nearby Arion Hall. (Kendra Lucht photo)

President of the Provisional Government Sanford B. Dole (played by Steven Boggs) poses before ʻIolani Palace, a building that his illegitimately-conceived government will rename the "Executive Building." Former Chief Justice of the Kingdom of Hawaiʻi, a missionary descendant and once a friend of Queen Liliʻuokalani, Dole's participation in the overthrow of the monarchy was viewed by the Queen as a betrayal of her trust. Looking on (*left to right*) are Dallas Mossman Vogeler and Charles Kaʻaiʻai of Hui Naʻauao and playwright Victoria N. Kneubuhl. (*Star-Bulletin* photo by Craig T. Kojima)

Lt. Lucien Young (played by Burl Burlingame) commands a detachment of sailors through Honolulu to Mililani Street, ending their march at the former site of Arion Hall just as the U.S. troops of the *U.S.S. Boston* did 100 years earlier. (Elizabeth Pa Martin photo)

182

‘ONIPA‘A
FIVE DAYS
IN THE
HISTORY
OF THE
HAWAIIAN
NATION

1893-1993

CLOSING CEREMONY

As torchbearers enter 'Iolani Palace grounds for the closing ceremony, a yellow glow illuminates the site where the Hawaiian monarchy was overthrown on January 17, 1893. (Deborah Uchida photo)

Torchbearers move in a solemn procession down King Street as they approach the entrance to 'Iolani Palace grounds. (Deborah Uchida photo)

The statue of Kamehameha I glows in the night as students of Kamehameha Schools gather to sing their alma mater, "Sons of Hawai'i," after ceremonies closed on January 17, 1993 at the 'Iolani Palace. (*Star Bulletin* photo by Dennis Oda)

184

'ONIPA'A
FIVE DAYS
IN THE
HISTORY
OF THE
HAWAIIAN
NATION

1893-1993

Kū ka lau lama, **Many torches stand. In ancient days, many lighted bonfires were a sign of victory, a fitting tribute to this uniting of the Hawaiian nation. (*Advertiser* photo by Gregory Yamamoto)**

At the age of four, Elijah Kamoali'i Smith,
son of Leimomi Kalāhiki Smith, is the
youngest torchbearer to the spirit and
pride of a nation. (Deborah Uchida photo)

'ONIPA'A
FIVE DAYS
IN THE
HISTORY
OF THE
HAWAIIAN
NATION

1893-1993

Hawaiians of all ages demonstrate on the beach at the Hilton Hawaiian Village during President Clinton's July 1993 visit to the islands. The demonstrations caught Clinton's attention, bringing national awareness to the Hawaiians' desire for sovereignty. (*Advertiser* photo by Debra Booker)

(Following page) With
the Hawaiian flag a
proud reminder that the
Kingdom of Hawai'i was
once a sovereign nation,
internationally recog-
nized by countries
around the world as an
independent, constitu-
tional monarchy, Native
Hawaiians from Lā'ie,
Ko'olauloa, O'ahu arrive
at the front entrance to
the Leiopapa-a-
Kamehameha Building.
The group marched
across the island to
present a list of their
concerns to the Hawai'i
State Legislature on
Opening Day of the 1993
session.
(*Star-Bulletin* photo by
Gregory Yamamoto)

188

**'ONIPA'A
FIVE DAYS
IN THE
HISTORY
OF THE
HAWAIIAN
NATION**

1893-1993